Los Alamos
Experience

Los Alamos
Experience

by Phyllis Fisher

Foreword by Alan Cranston

Japan Publications Inc.

Published by JAPAN PUBLICATIONS, INC., Tokyo & New York

Distributors:
UNITED STATES: *Kodansha International/USA, Ltd., through Harper & Row, Publishers, Inc., 10 East 53rd Street, New York, N. Y. 10022.* SOUTH AMERICA: *Harper & Row, Publishers, Inc., International Department.* CANADA: *Fitzhenry & Whiteside Ltd., 195 Allstate Parkway, Markham, Ontario, L3R 4T8.* MEXICO & CENTRAL AMERICA: *HARLA S. A. de C. V., Apartado 30–546, Mexico 4, D. F.* BRITISH ISLES: *International Book Distributors Ltd., 66 Wood Lane End, Hemel Hempstead, Herts HP2 4RG.* EUROPEAN CONTINENT: *Fleetbooks, S. A., c/o Feffer and Simons (Nederland) B. V., Rijnkade 170, 1382 GT Weesp, The Netherlands.* AUSTRALIA & NEW ZEALAND: *Bookwise International, 1 Jeanes Street, Beverley, South Australia 5007.* THE FAR EAST & JAPAN: *Japan Publications Trading Co., Ltd., 1–2–1, Sarugaku-cho, Chiyoda-ku, Tokyo 101.*

First edition: September 1985

LCCC No. 85–060542
ISBN 0–87040–623–X

Printed in U.S.A.

Acknowledgment

It gives me great pleasure to thank the several persons who have generously helped in the making of this book. My husband, Leon Fisher, whose work took us to Los Alamos and who shared the experience, contributed recollections, read and checked the manuscript, and supported me through endless hours of struggling to write with pen, typewriter, and eventually word processor. My mother, Helen Kahn Geballe, saved my letters from Los Alamos and continually encouraged me to write about my experiences there. My son-in-law, Larry Slotnick, rescued me and the book time after time when I became hopelessly ensnarled in the word processor. My good friend, David Swain, whose constant encouragement made me feel the effort was worthwhile, spent endless hours reading and correcting the manuscript. My heartfelt thanks to them all.

I would like to acknowledge the support of others who gave of their time to read the chapters that follow and made constructive suggestions. Professor Benjamin Bederson was helpful in amplifying an incident that happened to him. My son, Dr. Robert Fisher, tracked down facts and figures at Los Alamos and collected photographs. Helpful suggestions were made by Dr. George Sandoz, Peggy Joseph, my son Dr. Lawrence Fisher, and his wife Valerie. My thanks to them all.

Senator Alan Cranston kindly read the manuscript and wrote a thoughtful and sensitive foreword. Hedy Dunn, director of the Los Alamos Historical Museum, helped me search through piles of photographs, hunt for maps, and assisted me in selecting photographs appropriate for the book.

I hope the book bears out their warm and supportive comments and assistance.

To all my heartfelt thanks.

P. F.

Foreword

This account of Phyllis Fisher's life at Los Alamos during the
secret development of the atomic bomb is highly personal—
warm-hearted, humorous, and sensitive—and at the same time
conscious of the wider meaning of events as they unfolded on
that high, remote plateau.

Her husband, Leon Fisher, was one of the young physicists
who helped develop the bomb. She was a social worker, the
mother of a two-year-old son. She did not know what was
being developed in the secrecy and isolation of Los Alamos
until just shortly before Hiroshima was destroyed.

Her book, based on letters and recollections, traces her
experiences on the "hill," her difficulties with regulations,
restrictions, and rumors, as well as with her husband's silence.
Her beautifully written account is leavened with delightful
humor, human insights, and poetic descriptions of scenes on
that enchanting and terrifying mesa. It ends with her trip to
Hiroshima about four decades later, where she saw for herself the terrible evidence of a cruelty men hoped they had
outgrown.

Her manuscript came across my Senate desk during a fierce
battle over the MX missile, just at the time the Administration brought its chief peace negotiator back from arms control
talks in Geneva to lobby for this weapon. Mrs. Fisher's book
is filled with similar ironies.

The dedicated efforts to achieve peace and victory through
the physicists' work at Los Alamos culminates in the bombing
of Hiroshima and Nagasaki. The war ends, but the scientists'
joy in victory is tempered by their horror at the awesome
human destruction and their fear that the human race may
never experience true peace and may never feel safe again.

Mrs. Fisher alludes to the debate that preceded the bombing and contemporary suggestions that the force be internationalized. The bombing of Hiroshima was the final act of World War II, but she asks the chilling question: Was it the first act of the cold war that was to follow?

She writes of her distress that Dr. J. Robert Oppenheimer, the brilliant, greatly admired director of the project at Los Alamos, failed to join the group of physicists who attempted to harness the terrible forces they had released. Oppenheimer maintained that scientists should not involve themselves in politics. Perhaps he rejected the best means they had at the time for putting the genie back in the bottle. In the view of many, this can only be accomplished by political means through arms control and the eventual outlawing of war.

Mrs. Fisher writes that her early upbringing in San Francisco ill-prepared her for the realities of our times. Her favorite childhood prayer ended with "Grant us peace, Thy most perfect gift," and "grant that the day will come when all men will recognize that they are brothers so that, one in spirit and one in fellowship, they shall be forever united before Thee."

Her book describes the plight of a young wife and mother in a world out of control. She was driven to write it out of an affection for the human race. It is an apology, a plea for peace.

We can all hope that something so horrible as Hiroshima is the very nightmare that may bring peace. There is no other option.

The book is compelling because of its grasp of the meaning of her experience—that she was part of the world's changing. The 6,000 men and women at Los Alamos changed the world in that place. There is no need to go farther back in history. The lesson for our time began in 1945 with the explosion at Alamogordo.

ALAN CRANSTON

Contents

Acknowledgment, 5
Foreword by ALAN CRANSTON, 7

1. The Cenotaph and the Mesa, 13

   The Cenotaph, 13
   The Mesa, 15
   The Misfit, 17
   December 7, 1941, 21

2. Shangri-La, 23

   The View from Albuquerque, 23
   First View of the "Hill", 28
   Welcome to P.O. Box 1663, 31
   Questions without Answers, 37
   Who Lived behind Barbed Wire?, 41
   Muddy Problems, 51
   Leon's Letter, 54

3. Friends on the Hill, 57

   Minnie, 60
   Margaret, 62
   Brad and Louise, 63
   The Thin Man, 64
   Richard, 67
   Bob's Courtship, 68

4. Looking Around, 71

   Dealing with the Outside World, 71
   A Look at the Past, 74
   A Visit to a Familiar World, 78
   Cabs, Trains, and Garbage Trucks, 83
   The First Americans, 87

5. Pregnant Thoughts, 93

   Spreading the News, 93
   Coping with Secrecy, 97
   Mounting Tensions, 100

6. The Climax, 111

   Trinity, 111
   The Mushroom Cloud, 115
   The Local Newspaper, 118
   The Reaction on the Hill, 121
   Two Mischief Makers, 123
   The Wall of Silence, 127

7. Peace at Last, 131

   Hopes and Fears, 131
   A Manageable Crisis, 134
   Our Own Little War, 136
   Crossroads, 138
   Reward for a Job Well Done, 142

8. Harvest Time, 149

   Neighborhood Doings, 149
   Thanksgiving Warmth, 154
   Winter's Chill, 158

Festivities, 166

9. Learning New Lessons, 169

    A New School Principal, 169
    Babes in Arms, 172
    Babes in Washington, 176
    "Lost Almost", 178
    Another Education, 181

10. On Our Own, 185

    Risky Ventures, 185
    Violence, 190
    Farewells, 192
    Stripes are Back, 196
    Holiday Time on the Hill, 197
    Our World Widens, 200
    Humpty Dumpty, 206

11. Transients, 211

    Vacation on the Brink, 211
    Good-bye, 214
    Hello, 219
    Looking Eastward, 221
    Looking Westward, 225
    Farewell, Los Alamos, 227

12. Hiroshima—1979, 233

    Unfinished Business, 234
    The Letters, 239

    Postscript: Los Alamos, April 1983, 245
    Photographic Epilogue, 251

1. The Cenotaph and the Mesa

The Cenotaph

LITTLE LADY OF HIROSHIMA, you and I have never met. I was just a few yards behind you as we both approached the Cenotaph at the Peace Park in Hiroshima one cold November day in 1979. You were tiny, stooped and frail. The dark jacket you wore over your grey kimono made you seem all the more bent. In your hand you carried a spray of small chrysanthemums. Quite unaware of me, or of anyone else, you approached the Cenotaph and stood silently before it. Many had preceded you to this spot, for the jars in front of the monument already held many flowers. Slowly, you leaned forward and added your small contribution to one of the containers. Then, stepping back and standing more erect, you clapped your hands twice and bowed your head in prayer.

I stood behind you as you prayed. In the chill of that November day, I felt a shiver run through me, a chill that was followed immediately by a sudden surge of warmth toward you. As you stood amidst a scene commemorating "man's inhumanity to man," your quiet faith reached out to me. I wanted to reach out to you in response. I wanted to put my arms around you, to comfort you, and, perhaps at the same time, to comfort myself. I wanted to tell you that, as an American woman, I grieved with you. I wanted to say, "I'm sorry," and to add, "I, too, am a survivor."

Sorry? Why did I want to apologize? Why did that word

come to my mind? *I* didn't build the bomb that destroyed your world. Nor did I make the decision to use it. I certainly had nothing to do with the decision to target your city. A survivor? *Am* I a survivor? Not by any measure am I a survivor in the sense that I felt you must be. Your land was devastated, not mine. The war did not touch my homeland. Your life was shattered, not mine. I lost no one near or dear to me. But, in a very significant way, Hiroshima changed my life, too.

I wondered about you as you prayed. Were you involved in some way with the war effort in Hiroshima? Or had you lived in your community (as I had at Los Alamos), as a wife and mother, trying to manage through very difficult and fearful times, much more difficult for you, of course, than for me? What had happened to your husband and to your children? Did you, perhaps, believe that they died in a great and glorious cause? Or are you still numb from your losses, forever asking the question "Why?"

In the quiet of that late autumn day, I gazed at the trunk-like stone chest in front of both of us. I had learned that it contains the names of all who are known to have been killed by the atomic bomb that obliterated Hiroshima in August of 1945. I also knew that names are still being added to the chest's already long list, as the death toll from that horrible weapon continues to climb.

My attention was then drawn to the Cenotaph that arches over the chest, and the shape of the Cenotaph transfixed my thoughts. It is a starkly simple monument made of concrete and it stands about thirteen feet tall. It has steep sides, which incline slightly, and an almost flat top. How strange that it should be that shape!

The Mesa

As I observed the contour of the Cenotaph, my mind flew back
many, many years. I found myself recalling a barren, for-
bidding land mass of quite similar shape, flat on top and
surrounded by very high cliffs that descend sharply to the
valley below. I was picturing the view of Los Alamos, New
Mexico, from the desert beneath it, as I had first seen it.
This was the isolated, inhospitable location that had been
selected as the temporary home of the military-scientific
effort to create the weapon that destroyed both Hiroshima
and Nagasaki.

I knew that area well. For two very crucial and upsetting
years, from October 1944 to September 1946, I lived with
my husband and young son on that barren plateau high above
the desert. There, my physicist husband was part of the
scientific group that worked, in secrecy, on the development
of the bomb that forever changed your world, little lady of
Hiroshima.

I shared the wartime sense of excitement and dread that
permeated the whole isolated community of Los Alamos.
I was part of that thrilled and horrified community which
learned, on August 6, 1945, that its creation, the atomic
bomb, had been dropped on your city.

And now, I have seen your city and the grim evidence of
the disaster that befell it. I shall never forget you or the history you symbolize for me. However, I can only guess your
story. If, through some miracle of communication, we had
been able to understand one another's language, what would
we have said to each other? We would have met, not as representatives of a victorious and of a vanquished nation, but
simply as two women who grieve. Even so, could we have
bridged the gap between us? Could we have traversed the
distances of homeland, of history, of language and culture
that separate us? Could we have talked of war and of peace,
of your family and of mine, or our lives during those fateful

years, and of our hopes and fears for the future? It would
have been a most difficult conversation for us both. You have
experienced a nuclear disaster; I live in fear of one.

In a subtle way Los Alamos changed my world too, for
I have never lost the sense of helplessness I felt so strongly
that day, August 6, 1945.

Even so, I could not imagine at that time how thoroughly
the bomb that leveled Hiroshima and covered its rubble, its
dead and its suffering multitudes with a mushroom-shaped
cloud, was to change all our lives. I could not fully understand
what the release of nuclear energy was going to mean to all
of us in the years to come. Least of all could I comprehend,
so long ago, how the sinister shadow of that ominous cloud
would follow us to this day. In fact, I don't think I fully
realized all this until that chilly November day, in 1979,
when I stood a few yards behind you at the Cenotaph.
Perhaps it was in that sense that when I saw you I labeled
myself a "survivor," a survivor of the prenuclear age when
we both had at least the illusion of eventual safety and the
hope of a future for our children.

For me, those years when my husband and I lived at Los
Alamos framed a period of time that I have tried to push out
of my consciousness—without success. But now I would like
to share with you my experiences during that period. In
order to do this I shall draw from the many letters (over one
hundred) I wrote to my parents from Los Alamos, letters
they carefully saved. Naturally, these letters did not tell the
whole story. Mail leaving Los Alamos passed through military censorship. Additionally, as I wrote I was influenced by
my desire to protect my parents from unnecessary worry.
I felt I must hide or play down the depth of dismay and
depression I sometimes felt during that time. Upon rereading
my letters, I find that I did not succeed too well in hiding
my anxieties. Clearly, I was no heroine, but just a young
wife who wanted only to be a nest-builder and keep my little
family together. But who could build a nest with any safety

or permanence in the strangely fascinating and terrifying environment in which I found myself living at Los Alamos?

Before I share these letters and fill in for you a great deal that the letters did not tell, I should acquaint you with myself and my husband and share some of my recollections of the world of our childhood and youth.

The Misfit

In 1944, when Leon and I went to Los Alamos, I was a young, immature wife. Moreover, I was, in my own way, very provincial. I had grown up in San Francisco, California, protected and nurtured in a world of warmth, hope and economic security. My parents, descendents of families who had moved west many years before, felt privileged to live in San Francisco—and so did I. Looking back now, however, I realize that I was ill-prepared for the realities of our times. As a young Jewish child, I had learned in synagogue and home " . . . they shall beat their swords into plowshares, their spears into pruning hooks." My favorite prayer ended with "Grant us peace, Thy most perfect gift," and "grant that the day will come when all men will recognize that they are brothers so that, one in spirit and one in fellowship, they shall be forever united before Thee." I had learned in school that the "war to end wars" (World War I) had been fought and won. This early education meshed neatly with the values with which I had been nurtured. I believed in these ideals and acted on my early training in my daily life. I don't mean to imply that they were wrong as ideals, only that, in a way, they sheltered me from many harsh realities.

Reality, however, has a way of making itself unmistakably clear. One massive input from the world of reality, at that time, was the great economic depression of the 1930s. It was impossible not to be painfully aware of the fear and disillusionment that enveloped everyone as families suddenly lost their financial security, as banks closed, and as the growing ranks of the unemployed looked futilely for work that did not exist. The depression led to an increase in alcoholism, crime and suicide. It also led to a search on the part of thoughtful people for a utopian economic and social system that might control our economy and provide for all of us. Franklin Delano Roosevelt's election to the presidency of the United States in 1932 was an expression of that hope.

I was a student in junior high school when Roosevelt became our president. His sense of confidence was contagious, and the governmental programs he initiated held out the promise of mitigating our debilitating, nationwide impotence. Like many school children, I responded to his enthusiasm. It was cheering to believe along with our president that proper planning could accomplish miracles.

I became socially and politically aware in the years at school that followed. The University of California at Berkeley offered a plethora of courses devoted to the causes and amelioration of social problems. Avidly, I studied social economics. My interest lay in problems of racial minorities, the poor, and migrant workers. Underlying all my studies and activities was the conviction that there were no problems that could not be solved.

I wanted to learn and I wanted to help. My extracurricular activities were devoted to understanding and helping relieve interfaith and interracial problems. In graduate school, I sought specific focus and specialized skill, studying psychiatric social work and learning to help emotionally disturbed children, troubled marriages, and dysfunctional families. In more general terms, I was interested in opening communication between hurting, troubled people.

I had known Leon Fisher since my high school days. Born in Canada, Leon was the son of immigrants from Roumania. He had known poverty and deprivation during his childhood. He had always excelled academically. His career, too, led him to the University of California at Berkeley. When we married, I was working towards my Master's degree in social welfare and Leon was completing his research for his Ph.D. degree in physics. In an important way, his circumstances also gave him a sense of rational rapport with the social processes. His college career was completely financed by scholarships, fellowships, and teaching assistantships. This was evidence to both of us that at least part of the social system worked well, making it possible for deserving students to acquire appropriate knowledge and skills.

Our personal plans and aspirations did not reflect all that was happening in the world beyond the university. In fact, while we were both seeking pragmatic approaches to our lives and careers, much of the world was being moved by sinister forces. While we studied, communication was breaking down all over the world. The collapse of worldwide understanding and reasonable hopes for social cohesion and harmony was particularly evident in a form of irrationality and cruelty rising out of Germany. Though spawned in part by the depression, it became an evil in itself, far more threatening to human destiny than was the global economic depression. Whatever our problems in America, there was no way to ignore the rise of Hitler, accompanied by militarism, threats of conquest, and virulent anti-Semitism. Soon, there was no way to ignore the military expansion of the Third Reich as war began spreading throughout Europe.

Most Americans traced their roots to Europe. Consequently, the victories of the Third Reich concerned them deeply. The Nazis were an ever-expanding nightmare that threatened the entire world. My own German-Jewish heritage made me feel doubly appalled and personally vulnerable as I learned that our co-religionists were being sent to concentration camps. The ominous stories of extermination and plunder coming out of Germany could not be ignored or "planned away."

It wasn't a happy time for us when we learned that the Germans had negotiated an alliance with Japan. We reacted with a mixture of shock and amusement upon learning that the Germans suddenly considered the Japanese to be "Aryans, too." The growth of a militaristic, aggressive Japan had been, for many years, a matter of relatively minor concern to us. Most Americans, it must be admitted, knew little or nothing about the tremendous economic and social problems of the vast Orient. For many of us at the university, our picture of Japan was a composite of Puccini's *Madama Butterfly* and of Gilbert and Sullivan's *The Mikado of Japan*. We didn't feel personally involved in the problems of this distant group of small islands far across the Pacific. The same could be said about our ignorance of and indifference to the incomprehensively vast, heavily populated area of China that Japan had conquered. Initially, our vague hope was that the problems in that part of the world would quiet down somehow. It didn't matter very much how, so long as it didn't involve us.

But, as time went on, our uninvolvement became less likely and, finally, less possible. At the university, we began to follow Japan's expansionist military policies with growing concern. We were disturbed by (and argued vehemently against) scrap-iron shipments to Japan that might come back to us in the form of bullets. The escalation of concern affected our attitude toward Japan. We began to call the men of that country "Japs" and to regard them all as fanatics. We couldn't understand the people of Japan, couldn't measure Japanese logic by Western standards, or understand how an emperor could be considered a god. The revulsion felt toward the greater fascism in Europe transferred easily to the newly recognized fascism in the Orient.

Japan occupied northern Indochina in 1940. The joint Vichy France and Japanese occupation and administration of all of Indochina, starting in July 1941, led the United States to react by freezing Japanese assets in the United States and invoking an oil embargo. Many of us felt that this American-imposed sea blockade of Japan, which had been intended to force Japan to behave, instead would force that country into war—and it did.

December 7, 1941

On December 7, 1941, my parents and I were going over wedding plans as we waited for Leon to join us. He arrived, ashen-faced, and told us the dreadful news he had just heard. We turned on our radio and learned of the Japanese attack at Pearl Harbor. I felt sickened and frightened, but I can't remember feeling an intense surge of patriotism. I only wanted my loved one to be safe. Our wedding was to take place just two weeks later.

When Japan attacked Pearl Harbor on December 7, 1941, it ended our supposed national isolation and signaled for my country the beginning of World War II. A day later Germany, which had a mutual defense pact with Japan, declared war on the United States. From that date on, we were all inescapably involved in a war in both Europe and the Pacific.

Leon and I were married on December 21, 1941, just two weeks after Pearl Harbor, and went to live in a tiny apartment in the Berkeley hills. From our windows we could see the blacked-out city below us. News in the papers and on the radio was censored. We were very aware of our feelings of helplessness and vulnerability.

It was almost automatic, unfortunately, for a country that too often viewed social problems in racial terms, to label the war in the Pacific a conflict between the "Caucasian Americans" and the "yellow Japs." It didn't seem to matter that not all Americans were white. Quickly and tragically, Japanese-Americans in California were herded into internment camps as panic helped steer our nation's course.

Local draft boards now were routinely "selecting" those young men who would serve our country in the armed forces in Europe, Africa, and Asia. This led to a subtle change in the way many young American students viewed their government. The welcomed "New Deal" of the 1930s had, in their opinion, given way to a most unwelcome "raw deal" of the 1940s. Utopia had not arrived. Instead, the lives of our young men were at the mercy of the omnipotent draft boards and their grimly necessary military game of "Russian roulette."

I found myself overwhelmed by the cumulative effects of worldwide economic depression, growing fascism, and, in Europe, genocide with all the fear-bred responses. All over the world, war was raging. Destruction replaced construction, and the slogans of hate—man against man, race against race, ethnicity against ethnicity—obliterated messages of caring and of reconciliation.

This philosophy of caring and reconciliation that I had nurtured since my childhood seemed no longer to have much value. How could families be taught mutual support and understanding while the family of nations was busy murdering each other? Clearly my philosophy did not fit the tenor of world events. Where was the place, in wartime, for the idealist or for the pacifist? I was out of step with my times and, the truth is, have been ever since.

2. *Shangri-La*

The View from Albuquerque

THE YEAR 1944 saw a turning point in the war, in both
Europe and the Pacific. The Normandy invasion in
June, coupled with the Russian offensive on the eastern
front, had Germany clearly retreating. Japan, no longer ex-
panding, was actually relinquishing its conquests one after
one, but only after desperate battles.

We were living in Albuquerque, New Mexico, at the time.
Leon, twenty-six, and the possessor of a brand new Ph.D.,
was an instructor in the physics department at the University
of New Mexico. I was twenty-five and was working part-
time as a social worker in an adoption agency. Our son
Bobby was growing rapidly and was, to his adoring parents,
a most delightful baby.

Fortunately for us, our lives up to this point had been mini-
mally affected by the war. A year before, when we were
living in Berkeley, several faculty and graduate student
physicists had "disappeared" mysteriously. They could be
contacted only through a postal box number somewhere in
New Mexico, the state in which we now lived. Others of our
friends were serving with the military forces in either Europe
or Asia. Many wives and fiancées were waiting anxiously at
home for word of their men overseas. So far, we were lucky,
although we wondered how long our luck would last. Each
man between ages nineteen and twenty-six had to register at
a local draft board. Leon had registered in San Francisco
before we were married. At first, his draft board had considered his graduate student status and later his university

position as an acceptable and appropriate basis for his defer-
ment from military service. We knew, however, that his
status was always at risk. At any time he could be drafted and
sent to war.

One day early in October 1944, Leon received a letter
from Professor C. D. Shane, a professor of astronomy at the
University of California at Berkeley. The letter, which was
mailed from P.O. Box 1663, Santa Fe, New Mexico, offered
Leon a position to work with the Corps of Engineers. Leon
responded by telephone as requested in the letter. Then he
made immediate plans to move to the project. It seemed like
a veritable "bolt out of the blue" to me. I hadn't been consulted at all! Where it was, why it was or what it was—I did
not know. It was abundantly clear to me that neither of us had
any choice. Alerting my parents to our plans while attempting
to hide my dismay and make light of my ignorance, I wrote
on October 4, 1944:

> We're moving! Believe me, you're not any more sur-
> prised than I am! You'd like to know where we're going?
> So would we! And it isn't that Lee won't tell me. It's hard
> to believe, but he doesn't know either. The only encour-
> aging thing he could say was that we'll know where we
> are when we get there. Great!
>
> Lee came home from the university early this afternoon,
> tossed his briefcase on the couch and said, "Sit down, Phyllis,
> we've really got to talk." He was so serious that he
> ignored Bobby, who had toddled across the floor to greet
> him. He told me of an important phone call that he had
> made earlier in the afternoon, which really leaves us no
> choice and which will result in our making this sudden
> move.
>
> Here's what I *can* tell you. We'll be going "there" next
> week (less than a day's trip from Albuquerque) to select
> our living quarters, and we will move "there" sometime
> between the 26th and 30th of this month. We have been

directed to drive to a certain city and report to an incon-
spicuous address where we will be given further instructions. It's alright with me, so long as we're not met by a
bearded mystic, given a piece of thread and instructed to
follow it to its end. At this point, though, nothing would
surprise me.

We'll be able to write to you from "there" and you can
write to us. Our address will be a box office number in, I
think, Santa Fe, which isn't where we'll be living. If your
head is spinning as you read all this, just remember, so is
mine. I just stopped typing and reread this much of the
letter, and decided what your reaction to it must be. I'll
bet you're convinced, Mom, that I've gone completely mad,
and that these are the ravings of the insane. Dad, you're
the more practical one and you, doubtlessly, suspect that
we are now fugitives from justice who are going to hide in
the woods and subsist on berries until the cops forget
about us.

Bobby is taking it like a little man. I told him we were
leaving for somewhere else. He burped quietly, said "gda,"
and went on trying to get his left shoe on his right foot—
which already had a shoe on it. I told Fawn, and I think he
was simply delighted, but then our silly puppy always is
wild with enthusiasm when shown any attention at all.

For the time being, let's call the place Shangri-La or
Sh-La for short. I'm tired of writing "there" and "the
place," and I don't know what to call it. I couldn't tell you
its real name if I knew it. Please don't say anything to
anyone yet, at least until I tell you what you can or should
say. I'll write all I can about Sh-La. Please understand
that if I don't answer your questions, there is a reason. I
have been told that our mail, both incoming and outgoing,
will be censored. If my letters have less coherence than
usual, please blame it on the rules and regulations of our
future home.

Well, here we go, two so-called adults, one baby and

one fox-terrier, heading off to play "hide and seek" for the
duration. I'm pretty excited about it, but I'm frightened
too. It's very much like stepping off into space and I just
hope we land on our feet.

Shangri-La was the name of a strange, hidden, magical
mountain community where time stood still, so fascinatingly
described by James Hilton in his book *Lost Horizon*. It
seemed strangely appropriate for me to use this name for my
new home-to-be. I was not connecting it to the announced
mythical, secret starting place for the bombing raid over
Tokyo on April 18, 1942. Nor was I anticipating that I
might someday think of my own Shangri-La as another "Lost
Horizon."

But what was my Shangri-La going to be like? I had felt a
sudden sense of isolation and anger when I discovered that
Leon either wouldn't or couldn't answer my questions, of
which I had asked a great many. I was dumbfounded! Why
was it necessary to go there? Why couldn't I be trusted?
Trusted with what? We were going off to live in isolation
and "we" meant both of us! Why couldn't I know why? I
was no physicist and I wouldn't understand a detailed and
technical explanation, nor was I asking for specifics. In the
past, Leon had always patiently described his scientific projects or research to me. But this time he made it absolutely
clear that I wasn't to ask and, if I did, he wasn't about to
answer. I didn't like the implications, not at all! I felt uncomfortable, sensing a new distance between us, one that
might grow larger with the passage of time.

Then, too, we had lived in Albuquerque only seven months.
I had just begun to feel at home with the high desert land
and with its Spanish and Indian (Native American) population. At first, the desert surrounding Albuquerque had
appeared to us to be nothing more than a dusty, barren
wasteland, but it had begun to take on a color and a fascina-
tion of its own. We had explored as much of the country-

side as gas rationing had allowed, sampled a few Indian pueblos and surveyed ruins of the early conquistadores (Spanish conquerers). We began to appreciate the color and charm of these people in contrast to the bland, characterless-ness of the more recent Anglo (white) community that super-imposed countless identical markets, hamburger stands, and "five-and-ten-cent stores" on this unique and, to me, almost foreign land. We had made new friends whom we liked. I had just started working part-time. Life in Albuquerque was just beginning to become interesting. There seemed to be little incentive for me to move away to a place about which so little information was forthcoming.

And now, so soon, we were to leave the gentle rhythm of this little town of 35,000 and exchange it for a mountain settlement that was cut off from the rest of the world. What would it be like? Why the secrecy? A battery of anxious questions from my parents did not help. How could I give them the answers to questions Lee wouldn't answer for me? And I wrote:

Authoritative books on child-rearing warn me that when Bobby is three (or is it four?) he'll ask countless questions, many of them unanswerable. Well, it will take him a full year to ask as many questions as you did in your last letter. The worst of it is, I can't answer anything! I don't *know* the answers and I couldn't tell you if I *did*! No, we can never give you the size of the project. They take precau-tions that this information not be known. For example, we have been told not to transfer what they flatteringly term our "entire bank account" to a bank nearer the project. And, "What kind of work will Leon do?" and "Is it dangerous?" Mom! How can I answer you? Then you ask, "Can you assure us you will stay in New Mexico or, at least in continental U.S.A.?" I can tell you're both worried. I don't know what to say to you.

My irritation over our prospective move vanished, however, after a preliminary visit to our future home.

First View of the "Hill"

Heading north from Albuquerque, we passed miles of empty desert and bare hills. Then we followed a dirt road that took us up through steep, colorful canyons to a rocky plateau. On the way, the road curved and careened past huge formations of reds and golds that appeared to be immense blocks of stone left over from eons ago, possibly from the time of the creation of the world. Moreover, this area, so new and strange to me, didn't look quite finished.

Once up on the plateau, we saw that the land dropped off almost perpendicularly on three sides. Land this shape is commonly called a mesa. Mesa is a Spanish word meaning table, in this case table-shaped land. Our mesa was a tongue of land flat on top and connected to the mountain range to the west (and thus, technically, a potrero).

At the dizzying altitude of 7,300 feet, the air was clear and crisp, and the sun was brilliant. It didn't bother us, at first, that the site consisted of army prefabs and quonset huts that seemed to have been dropped helter-skelter on the barren earth. The homes were minimal, to be sure, and dirt roads gridironed the living area. But, the view—the view from the mesa to the east—was nothing short of breathtaking! Before us stretched the broad valley of the lazy Rio Grande dotted with Indian villages, some farmlands, a few scraggly cottonwood trees, and not much else. Beyond the valley, rose the magnificent Sangre de Cristo (Blood of Christ) mountain range with towering peaks that were already snow-covered. To the west, behind our flat, rocky, future home rose the equally majestic Jemez mountain range. It mattered little to us that most of the mesa was treeless, for just to the rear of the huts and technical buildings there stretched a forest of ponderosa pine—rather scraggly in the opinion of *this* Californian, but a forest nevertheless.

It occurred to us that the steep-sided mesa surrounded by virtually empty countryside had the appearance of a natural fortress, but even that didn't dampen our spirits. We found a busy and exciting world where lively young adults and small children seemed to be thriving in the exhilarating mountain air. My comments to my parents in my letter home mirrored our initial enthusiasm, as well as our relief that Leon would be working in a place where his expertise could be used. This should mean that we would not have to be separated by the military draft. As I wrote home on October 11, 1944:

I'm breathless! We've been "there"! Shangri-La is super! We drove up yesterday and stayed just long enough to tour the place, pick out our house and learn some of the rules, regulations and by-laws of this Never-Never-Land. Naturally, the day was not uneventful. In fact, Lee and I are still blushing over our latest butch.

I wrote you that we were given an address in Santa Fe from which we were to receive further instructions. We dutifully followed our little map, found the address alright and stared at it in amazement. The place was a bakery! Once in, we didn't know what to do. A girl behind the counter asked if she could help us and we boobs were tongue-tied. Lee finally stated that we were "told to come here." Silence reigned. More silence. Believe me, I fully expected the girl to break open a loaf of bread, surreptitiously extract from it a message written in code and slyly slip it to us. Instead, a bored voice from the other side of the room said, "You must be looking for the office down the way; people are going in and out of there all the time." We felt like four cents, said our thanks and meekly ambled out. Fine beginning! The office down the way was presided over by Dorothy, a genial, relaxed woman from whom we learned that we were expected and were given our directions to Sh-La. Then we started out on a most spectacularly beautiful drive.

Shangri-La is a streamlined, alpine settlement, size unmentionable, location unmentionable, altitude unmentionable. But it's very complete. We found theater, sports field, playground, and a school. There is even a radio station that picks up programs and adds music. Apparently, we will live in a spot where ordinary radio reception is extremely poor.

Anyway, the inmates assure us that there is plenty here to compensate for the very extreme isolation. We saw notices of picnics, dances, bridge parties, etc. If we get tired of my cooking, and that's entirely possible, we can eat out at the mess hall. We are entitled to use the Army commissary and PX, and they seem quite adequate.

Lee and I were lectured briefly on the importance of developing an anti-social outlook. We're not to be friendly with residents of nearby towns. (I hadn't noticed any nearby towns.) If we go to Santa Fe (which isn't my idea of nearby) we are to keep to ourselves and not talk to outsiders unless it is necessary in the transaction of business, etc. However, we are allowed a half-smile and a slight nod to persons we already know there. "Only this and nothing more."

Rents are proportional to salary, 10 percent, I think, having nothing to do with the size or location of the house. The number of rooms allotted is determined only by the size of the family. I wish I could write that the homes are lovely white colonial cottages or Spanish haciendas. They seem to come in three styles, roughly designated by me as barracks, garages, and crackerboxes. We had our choice and selected one of the crackerbox variety, a little square thing consisting of lots of windows surrounding practically nothing. We'll have two small bedrooms, living room, and kitchen. Maid service is prorated according to the size of one's family. We rate one half-day a week and were told seriously that if we want more help we'll have to have another baby. Housing is, obviously, the same story. A larger family rates a larger house, and *no* increase in rent! Interesting, huh? Tempting? We'll see.

Medical care seems very adequate and, best of all, is completely free. There is a small hospital here (which looks like barracks) and it seems well staffed. Moving should be comparatively simple. The housing office forwarded a floor plan of our future home, so I can determine ahead of time just where each piece of furniture will be placed. We'll be very comfortable once we're settled.

Just noticed that I misdated this letter. It is now, and has been for three minutes, October 12. And way past my bedtime.

Welcome to P.O. Box 1663

Soon after writing that enthusiastic letter about Sh-La, we made the move to Los Alamos. Every step of the way we encountered surprises, as was reflected in my October 27, 1944 letter:

We've moved! We're here, and you should see us! Boxes, boxes, boxes everywhere. Bobby is asleep on the front seat which we removed from our car and placed strategically between the laundry hamper and my sewing machine. And why isn't our little towhead snuggled cozily in his own little beddie? Because we simply cannot dig down through the pile of debris that was and will be the makings of our happy home, to uncover the slats of our baby's crib!

It had all seemed so *organized* when we started off. I had given the movers the floor plan of our supposed future home and marked on it just where each piece of furniture

should be placed. Moreover, I had put labels on every
piece of furniture designating its assigned spot. We were
off in a blaze of glory and I anticipated a very easy job of
getting started.

Our trip to Santa Fe was uneventful, which was fine.
But, there were endless delays at the office-with-the-same-
address-as-the-bakery, necessary ones, I suppose. Among
other things, it was discovered that one of the two movers
lacked the proper credentials (he had no draft registration
card, and promptly disappeared when asked to produce one).

You can tear up the floor plan I sent you. Any resemblance between it and the place we're living in is purely
coincidental. Our belongings were unceremoniously dumped
in the wrong house, a smaller place (classification: garage
style) at about six o'clock this evening. Our chosen home,
we were told by a WAC [Women's Army Corps member]
in the housing office, had been assigned by mistake to
someone else. Instead, after a great deal of scurrying
around, we were deposited *here* to remain until another
batch of houses can be built. The WAC tried to be comforting, assuring us in her most languid southern accent,
that it would be but a week or so before these next prefabs
would be tossed together, and we could move.

As I told you, we arrived here with one mover missing.
Then the lone, remaining mover decided to express himself. Seems he "didn't feel so good," thought the altitude
was affecting him, felt just a wee bit woozy, but didn't
want to complain, or anything like that. Then our WAC
added, helpfully, that it would be nice, she thought, to get
some laborers, but it was by now well after working
hours on Saturday and no one was available to help empty
the moving van until the following Monday. Then she
drifted off. Well, " 'I'll do it myself,' said the little red
hen" or rather, in this case, the red-with-rage rooster!
And he did!

Lee started unloading our washing machine, our steamer

trunk, etc., with our wilted mover gingerly lifting a finger to assist him now and them. And it would be then that Bobby set up a terrible roar. He had suddenly decided that he was doomed to starvation. Lee suggested helpfully, from under the headboard of our bed, that I feed Bobby. I would have been delighted to, but our box of food was still to appear from the depths of the truck. The store here was closed, and, and, and, and . . . . oh, *HELP!*

Fortunately for us, the couple who share this duplex with us heard the racket and came out to investigate and introduce themselves. Bonnie, a sweet-looking blonde, offered to feed Bobby, and her husband Avery started helping Lee unload. The driver's assistance, at this point, had been reduced to feeble advice.

What lifesavers Bonnie and Avery were. In no time, Bonnie had Bobby fed, cleaned and happy, and asleep on her bed. Avery showed us how to light the heater in the living room (after pushing everything to a safe distance) and introduced us to the intricacies of our stove which, I learned to my horror, burned only wood and coal. The coal, I learned later, was of such a poor grade that it was useless anywhere else. The residents here call the stove "black beauty" because black is what it is and beauty is is what it isn't.

Then we left Bobby with our neighbors (I've never left my baby with anyone on such short notice!) and staggered off in search of dinner. Naturally we got lost in the dark but finally found the coffee shop and filled up on tasteless hamburgers and horrible coffee. Upon our return we removed the car seat from our car, collected Bobby and placed him on it for the night. Now, it only remains for us to figure what we'll do for food until the commissary opens on Monday and a few other trivial things like that!

I still think I'll like it here. Does my voice sound just a wee bit shaky?

It was not a good beginning, but we determined to make the best of it. First, we decided to unpack as little as possible and devote our time, for the present, to exploring our area and meeting our co-isolates. We assembled Bobby's crib, unpacked what we had to, and left it at that, to the delight of Bobby and Fawn. The two of them had a great time climbing over, under, and through the collection. When Bobby napped, Fawn snoozed on a couch pillow wedged between our large suitcase and the laundry hamper. At that time I would head for the typewriter, which was perched precariously on a carton, and, sitting sideways, continue my letters to my parents in order to make good my promise that I would tell them all I could about Shangri-La.

Yesterday, Lee with Bobby on his shoulders and I with Fawn at my heels did a little exploring. The country here is unbelievable! The forests of pine remind me of the high Sierra country, but of that country gone completely mad. We strolled along a gentle mountain trail that curved through the trees and then came to an abrupt stop that left us staring down a sheer drop of over 500 feet. There are apparently many of these sudden cliffs and canyons in this area. And these incredible canyons far below give you the impression, somehow, that they are as surprised to be there as we are to discover them.

Lee and I wandered around again last night after Bobby was asleep. To say the least, it was b-r-r-r-isk out. We climbed through a "crackerbox" not yet completed. (Ours?) It was encouraging to see a row of semi-constructed dwellings. Oh, I'm sure we'll be moving in a very few days.

And, speaking of moving, Bobby has the moving bug, and it's so funny. He's determined to be helpful and he unpacks and packs everything in sight. I opened the hamper this morning and found the strainer and dish mop on top of the dirty clothes. He's been trying to stuff his

doll into one of the opened barrels. Then, he filled a wastebasket with some of his toys and dragged them around to
where we were unpacking kitchen essentials, emptied,
refilled and then chugged off somewhere else to repeat
the whole performance.

All day Sunday, we subsisted on charity. Neighbors all
around called, sympathized with us, and contributed what
they could spare. By noon on Sunday, we had added gifts of
milk, bread, canned vegetables, and three apples to our
box of staples. By three o'clock I had found our can opener
and so we dined sumptuously on the above items supple-
mented by a can of tuna we had brought along.

Well, it's time to start dinner. I find I can turn out a
very simple meal in a mere three hours or so, if I am
lucky. The problem of getting things to actually cook
hasn't been quite solved (because water boils at a lower
temperature at high altitude), but then, I've heard that
most foods are more nutritious served raw. Maybe we'll
subsist on berries yet, Dad. Viva La Guerre!

And a few days later:

Right now Bobby is trying to figure out how to put a
sweater on without assistance. Frankly, I think he's
struggling against overwhelming odds. He's been at it
about fifteen minutes now with grunts, gasps and acro-
batics and a stern request for no assistance—please! My
fingers are itching to straighten out the whole mess for
him. I know I should leave him alone and so I determined to
give my fingers a workout on the typewriter, instead.

Last night, we saw "Our Hearts were Young and Gay"
at the theater here. It's a good picture, at least, I *think* it is.
The first fifteen minutes are fine, even highly amusing,
but I'm no judge of the movie from that point on. I'm an
excellent judge, however, of the hard wooden benches
we sat on for the "duration." Sit back and relax? Hah!

There are no backs! And, even sit *down* with any degree
of comfort? Not me! I'm not, shall we say, well enough
upholstered to compensate for the strange type of wood
here, which I'm positive gets harder by the minute.

Have you ever used a mangle [a machine for ironing
material by inserting it between rollers]? I had my first
introduction to one today. Looked simple, was simple—to
others. Nothing to it. You just run things through it, I
was told, and sure enough, near me in the big community
laundry, I saw evidence of a neat load of ironing, or is it
mangling, and in "one quarter of the time." So I tried it
and what a mess! Things looked worse than when I
started. I was conscious of the amusement I caused and
felt embarrassed, for I could tell that it was only politeness
that kept them from laughing. Finally, I discreetly folded
my mangled belongings in a having-been-ironed fashion
and sneaked them home to my good, old-fashioned, done-
by-hand process.

And speaking of old-fashioned, there may be something
quaint and homey about a wood stove, but there is *nothing*
useful about our "black beauty." We rush into the kitchen
at about 6:00 A.M. full of high hopes and good spirits. I
stoke like wild; Lee manipulates the dampers hopefully.
The wood is green, cold, and uncooperative (often covered
with ice). At most, it steams along in a lackadaisical way.
At around 7:30, Lee leaves the house—hungry.

Finally this morning I really outdid myself. Threw
everything I could think of into the stove. Result? A
roaring blaze! Some of the bottom came off the frying pan
and stuck to the stove, which is no longer new and shiny
and now looks like the usual antique. The frying pan now
has a sandpaper bottom. Small sacrifice for a hot meal of
cooked cereal, eggs and steaming hot coffee. Pardon me for
boasting, but it's good for my morale.

Bravo! Bobby finally has the sweater on. Well, it's
upside-down, but it's *on*. His arms are in the sleeves

alright, but the rest of the sweater is around his shoulders.
He's strutting around proud as heck.

I'm doing some advance decorating for Bobby's room.
I covered the little toy box and the barrel and have enough
material left over for curtains. It's just slightly sissy in
design, but cheerful. I'll enclose a sample of the material.

Questions without Answers

As the days grew colder, my spirits warmed. I was learning
to cope. Still, settling down in our new home proved, in so
many ways, more difficult than I had anticipated, and a
constant barrage of questions from my parents didn't help.
I tried to sound cheerful but my irritability began to show.
I was aware of their concern but there wasn't much I could
do about it. I couldn't tell my parents at the time that they
were not the only ones plying us with questions and inno-
cently adding to our difficulties.

During that same week, a former colleague of Leon's got
our "P.O. Box 1663, Santa Fe" address and wrote to us. He
had been one of Dr. J. Robert Oppenheimer's graduate
students at the University of California at Berkeley. He
asked a number of direct, but unanswerable, questions about
the size and purpose of our project. He wondered if there
were a job opportunity for him here since he was not happy
where he was.

Leon took the matter to his division leader, Dr. Bacher,
who talked to Dr. Oppenheimer. Apparently, Oppie (Oppenheimer's nickname) did not approve of hiring our friend at
that time. Lee wrote a vague letter suggesting the matter be
dropped. It wasn't! Our friend wrote back an outraged letter.
He even mentioned Oppie in the letter without knowing that
Professor Oppenheimer was at the project, much less its
director. He ended the letter with a statement that he was
coming west by train. Could Leon meet him in Albuquerque,

possibly at the train station where they could talk things over? The result was that Leon was called in to the security office to explain the letter, and he was instructed, rather *commanded*, not to answer the letter at all. I almost wished I had been similarly instructed in regard to my parents' questions. Well, I hadn't been so instructed, so I wrote:

I felt a little guilty when you wrote, Mom, that Dad had just phoned you to tell you there was "a nice fat letter at the office from Phyl." I could imagine how you must have looked when you discovered that it was stuffed with samples of material for Bobby's room. Well, life is full of just such disappointments.

As I type, I'm munching on a CHOCOLATE CAKE THAT I BAKED! It isn't bad. Leon even ate it and he *never* does anything like that just to be polite. I made it in two installments in my pyrex frying pan (cake tins are down in the depths of one of the barrels) and tried to stack the lop-sided layers together with dubious success.

We were amused by your query as to our garden, which is nonexistent. Though our habitat is primitive, please don't grieve for us. The surrounding countryside more than makes up for lack of formal planting, and the views from our present "estate" are really beyond description.

While I'm at it, I'd better answer more of your questions:

1. In an emergency, we can phone out.

2. No, I don't need an umbrella.

3. Mom, please stop asking about Lee's work. Crossing the street is dangerous, too, you know.

4. No, I have no special announcement to make. I asked Sara [Leon's sister] to return the baby clothing I loaned her. I didn't want her to pass them on to anyone else. Anyway, we don't intend Bobby to be an only child.

5. No, I don't have any idea when we'll move. Neither has the contractor, and I've talked to him. He showed me

where our place will be. It's just a boggy patch of ground right now. Very discouraging. He scoffed at my heating worries, said the oil heater that we'll have is most adequate and that I'll be pleasantly surprised at its efficiency. Gee, I'll be pleasantly surprised to find any house there at all—ever!

And I do want to get away from this coal [used in this house's heater]. It's filthy. Our front yard is one big coal bin, and Bobby and Fawn get so black and then track it through the house. I mop every night.

The weather is cold now, and our friends tell us that they had snow here last year at this time. We can see some in the distance. The range across the valley is snow-capped and the sunset seems to turn it into luscious pink ice cream. (Now I know how that mountain range got its name!) Oh, Dad, please send me some slacks and a heavy sweater. I'll need them and soon. [My father was in the women's apparel business. Despite the war with its inevitable shortages, he often could find needed clothing.]

At first, I thought of Sh-La as a fortress. Certainly we were safe on our impregnable heights. A twelve-foot barbed-wire fence kept "them" out. K9 Corps dogs (K9 stands for "canine") patrolled the base of the cliffs that surrounded us and mounted police patrolled the heights. We had food, clothing, shelter, and each other. But gradually I began to suspect that *we* were the prisoners, the dangerous ones, and that "they" were the safe ones outside.

Why? Well, what sort of people are fingerprinted, photographed, and required to identify body scars upon arrival? We were! Who has mail censored? We did! Our incoming mail was opened and read by censors and then resealed. This led to delays of usually 48 hours. Outgoing mail was taken to the tech area (an abbreviation for the technical area that was surrounded by high barbed-wire fence and could only be entered by the bearer of an appropriate badge) by our husbands and deposited there unsealed. There, it was read by military censors, passed if approved, or, if not accepted, returned to us for rewriting with corrections. We had no phones in our living quarters, but could use one of several central public phones. We were allowed to phone home *only* from the project and outgoing calls were monitored. We could mail personal photographs of the immediate family. We were forbidden to send pictures of our friends or give their last names. In some cases, we couldn't reveal their real names at all. Delays seemed endless. Scientific journals were not mailed directly to us, but forwarded from our home addresses. We kept our old state automobile licenses and banked by mail to our pre-Shangri-La banks.

Up on our hill, we were told what we needed to know, period. Those who had white badges, Leon included, knew the details of the research going on. Those with blue badges knew what they needed to know for their part of it. And unemployed wives were to know nothing. Explosions could be heard daily. We knew weapons were involved, that was all. Moreover, the place I called Shangri-La didn't even exist as a military establishment. For example, if we tried to order something through the PX, we would find that there was absolutely no way to do it because, officially, there was no such hill or project.

All the above was food for thought as I climbed over and around our boxes and stoked our "black beauty." The suspicion that *we* were considered the threat or the danger to the outside world added a Kafkaesque, dream-like quality to our existence on the hill. This feeling of unreality was heightened for me by Bobby's delighted acceptance of the status quo and the occasional circus-like appearance of our house.

Bobby's little Mexican chair is back atop the big rocker again. That's where it landed and stayed the first few days here, so now, Bobby insists that's where it belongs. It's snowing in a half-hearted way outside, but inside it's cozy and warm. I'm so accustomed to the boxes and cartons heaped around that I hardly notice them. I've discovered that I can usually rest my eyes by looking up. But not today! I did a tremendous washing, got the clothes on my line, and filled Bonnie's line, too. And so, of course, it promptly began to snow. Now this place looks like a parade ground. I have ropes criss-crossed every which way and hung, or rather flagged, with Bobby's essentials which must get dry despite the weather. A few trained seals, an elephant or two, and I could charge admission.

In recognition of the thermometer's sudden and severe drop, the authorities have issued to the men some outer clothing which are humorously called "zoot-suits." Lee came home and modelled his today much to my amusement —and envy. The pants, very heavy and baggy, come up to Lee's chest and strap over his shoulders. Next, a huge heavy coat and the funniest cap with a sort of snood in the back and a very coy chin strap. Lee looks like an oversized cocker spaniel in a bathing cap.

Leon was also issued shatter-proof glasses and shoes that would conduct electricity. I couldn't mention these and didn't feel like joking about them. Not at all!

Who Lived behind Barbed Wire?

In a very short time Shangri-La began to take on a personality of its own. Nameless dirt streets and roads were located in reference to the water tower. One lived "north of the tower" or "east of the tower." The growing town quickly outstripped its limited water supply and also put a strain on an inadequate power supply. Housing continually lagged behind the population increase. There were, clearly, too many of us for our meager resources. And so the weathered and

worn water tower represented our point of reference as well
as our forlorn hopes for survival on our bleak mesa.

One got used to the nondescript, utilitarian green barracks
and buildings strewn about. We grew to appreciate the buildings left over from the Boys Ranch School that predated
Shangri-La as a military-scientific locale. That architecture
could only be labeled "early log cabin" and was strangely
appropriate as scenic backdrop for our pioneer existence. As
a matter of fact, one street *was* named, although the name
did not appear on any map. It was called "Bathtub Row" and
was the site of several log cabin-style buildings which were
unique in that they possessed bathtubs, the only bathtubs on
the hill.

In my mind, the residents of the hill began to sort themselves out into four separate groups. Preeminently, Los
Alamos was an Army post. The officers, for the most part,
were regular army personnel whose service predated the war.
The GIs had been taken out of combat units and most had
seen active duty overseas. Now, they were condemned to
stand guard, pick up garbage, and patrol a facility whose
purpose and function were unknown to them. A fine way to
win the war while their buddies were fighting and dying
overseas! To make matters worse, their job was to protect
scientists, civilian scientists, who didn't particularly care
about being protected. And so it was that the Army ran the
town.

One barracks near the west gate housed the SED (Special
Engineering Detachment) unit. These were also GIs, but
soldiers with a difference. Snatched quickly from academia and
drafted into the Army, these young men worked directly with
the scientists. Once on the hill, they had two aims in life:
first, to get as much scientific work as possible done; and
second, to pay as little attention to the military as they could
under the circumstances. They liked to sleep late and work
late in the familiar old academic manner. Generally they

were the bane of the befuddled MPs, who weren't allowed to know what the SEDs were doing.

Occasionally, there was a military "parade" on the hill. The MPs marched smartly along, followed by a group of smart-stepping WACs. Then came the SEDs, the most bedraggled group ever to don uniforms. Some slouched and some peered through thick eyeglasses as they ambled along. Whether fat, thin, short or tall, they were generally out of step and certainly out of military trim. Comically, each seemed to be out of step with all the others!

The scientists were the prima donnas of the mesa. In the first place, they had homes—muddy, drafty, and rudimentary, but homes. Their families came with them, to the envy of the enlisted men. Moreover, they were fiercely independent and strongly individualistic. They were largely city people and accustomed to simple comforts. They devoted long hours and a great deal of energy to research, and they worked under great tension and pressure. They, their wives, and families were temporary transplants from the universities, in partic- ular from the University of California at Berkeley, the Cali- fornia Institute of Technology, the University of Chicago, Columbia University, and Cornell University. Many of the scientists had been acquainted with each other prior to their arrival at Los Alamos. Many had worldwide reputations. A not inconsiderable number were from Europe.

Dr. Oppenheimer, or "Oppie," the scientific director, accomplished the miracle of forging this disparate group into a creative, cooperative force. He also worked closely with General Leslie Groves and the military command on the hill whose function was to see that the procurement of personnel and equipment and the maintenance of the site were properly expedited and at the least possible cost.

Then, there was the construction and maintenance staff; some of them lived on the hill. They had the poorest housing of all. They lived in corrugated metal quonset huts, which had minimal room separation and no insulation from heat or cold. There were never enough resident laborers, nor enough with the proper skills. So, daily, from the world outside came a bus with Indian and Spanish-American day-laborers as well as maids. In the late afternoon they vanished by bus to their homes in the valley below.

Although our promised housing hadn't materialized, the proffered household help had. As I wrote on November 9, 1944:

> I have household help today for the first time. She came to the house all rolled up in a bright red blanket and all smiles. She calls me "Meesie Feeshah" and tells me her name is "Apolonia." She is a short, middle-aged, stooped Indian woman from a nearby pueblo. She looks as though she couldn't lift a feather. But, whether or not she can clean the house is immaterial. I'm sure she'll be worth her wages in entertainment value alone. She is sweet and picturesque, and I love to watch her. If she does nothing more than stand around, I'll find my housework less boring.

Apolonia came faithfully one morning a week. She was happy to sweep and dust around our cartons. Sometimes she'd stop work and make little clay or paper toys for a delighted Bobby. There was one problem: she was afraid of anything run by electricity. We had acquired a clumsy, old washing machine. I'd drag it over to the sink, fill it with water, plug it in and, with its engine roaring, it did a fair job of cleaning the mesa dirt and coal dust off our clothing. Then a switch got the wringer rolling. I'd run it, and Apolonia watched over and over in amazement. I tried to encourage her to try to run the machine, which, after all, was pretty simple. Little by little, as weeks went by, she made cautious attempts. Finally, one day I connected the machine and encouraged her to start the wash while I went to the commissary. And, bravely, she went to work.

I returned to a weeping Apolonia and a mountain of suds pouring out of the churning machine. Quickly, I reached over and pulled out the electrical plug and, of course, the machine promptly stopped its volcanic activity. Through her tears, Apolonia whispered, "Meesie Feeshah *so* smart." From that day on, I washed; she watched.

Apolonia's regular appearance for a few hours on Thursday mornings was a reassuring sign that, to a certain extent, the ubiquitous military presence functioned at least partially in our behalf. However, just as the project had been planned and assembled in haste, similarly the rules and regulations governing Shangri-La were equally speedily and thoughtlessly thrown together. Sometimes it was necessary to find a way around rules that could not be abrogated and that made absolutely no sense to me. For example, this is what happened one stormy, miserable, early morning when I took Fawn to the veterinary hospital. The first trip there was uneventful—as far as the Army was concerned. But,

Yesterday I took Fawn to the vet's, and ever since, he has been the center of much unwanted attention, much to his disgust and discomfort. The vet gave him an enema which dislodged quantities of sticks and grasses. I thought that would be the end of our troubles, but in the evening he was limp and feverish. Lee looked at me, I looked at Lee. Finally he said, "Well, you'd better do it," and with an unhappy sigh, Lee wandered out into the night. So I did! Gave him an enema, that is. How I managed will not be related. Suffice it to say that the results were good. More grass arrived, if you're interested. Fawn seemed to feel a little better. I felt decidedly worse. Just when I had everything nicely cleaned up again, Lee showed up, looked the situation over, and expressed approval.

But, this morning Fawn was worse again. I started off (to the vet's) with Fawn in the car about 6:45 A.M. I had to go that early because Lee leaves for work at 7:30 A.M. I had to get back before he left. Why? Bobby, of course. The vet, sleepy but co-operative, gave me medication and we were ready for the return trip by 7:20. Then came the matter of the "Gate."

Now, listen to this very carefully and try to understand. I can't. We have a gate here that isn't a gate at all. It consists of a guardhouse and an unfriendly signpost surrounded by sentries. Regulations governing passage of said "gate" top any screwy regulations of any Army post anywhere. It seems that you can *drive* past it in an automobile without showing a pass, but you can't *walk* past it. Pedestrians must show passes. No exceptions.

I drove past the gate (to the vet's) with Fawn and, naturally, wasn't stopped. The veterinary hospital is only about 100 yards beyond and is visible from the gate. After our visit with the vet, I rushed out with my shivering dog, climbed into the car to start back, and—you guessed it— the car wouldn't start. By this time, it was snowing. I began to run as best I could, with Fawn held securely inside my coat. Of course, I was promptly stopped at the gate. I had no pass! In my rush to get Fawn to the vet's and back, I had neglected to take it. I explained to the sentries that my car wouldn't start. I had to get back. My husband *had* to get to work. My baby would be *alone*! My dog was *dying*! None of which made any difference. Only one word seemed to have meaning, the word "regulations." There were, it seemed, no provisions for someone who *drove* out the gate and had to *walk* back through it. Too bad. By then the snow was slanting and spinning angrily, and I wasn't getting any warmer. Fawn wasn't getting any lighter. They could see my car standing there, but that didn't make any difference. One MP suggested that I phone someone who could come out and identify me. Fine help! No one I knew had a phone. Lee couldn't be reached by phone until he left Bobby and went to work. And he wouldn't do that (I certainly hoped he wouldn't do that) until I was safely home What to do?

Then through the gloom and the swirling snow, there appeared a jeep, with driver, of course. Through chattering teeth, and right in front of the MPs, I asked the stranger for a lift. He agreed. I climbed into the jeep and in we went with full permission of the guards at the gate!

A few days later, with Fawn recovered, we had our first opportunity to become acquainted with the colorful world of some of the Indians who worked on our hill, and we looked forward eagerly to our trip. They came from the surrounding pueblos in the valley below—from Santa Clara, San Ildefonso, Tesuque, Pojoaque, and others. These pueblos, up to this point, were just names to me. The sturdy, good-natured Indians on our hill were a colorful sight. The women wore peasant-type blouses, and over them simple black garments that covered only one shoulder and fell to their knees. A bright yarn or beaded belt and leather moccasins completed the outfit. Their glossy black hair was usually folded back from their shoulders and tied tightly from the nape of the neck to the shoulder with brightly colored yarn. Over their foreheads, their front hair was cut neatly into bangs.

On November 13, with Bonnie, Avery, and two men who worked with Leon, we wound down the tortuous dirt road and visited our first pueblo.

I never dreamed that an Indian Pueblo could be so attractive. Tesuque is situated in the Rio Grande Valley, which lies between the Jemez and Sangre de Cristo ranges. The day was clear and crisp, and the sight of snow-capped mountain peaks above the roofs of the pueblo was really thrilling. This pueblo is very small and consists of squatty, thick-walled rows of pinkish adobe structures surrounding an open plaza where there is a covered, round building (kiva) that has some ceremonial purpose. The place was immaculate. Booths for the display and sale of pottery were everywhere.

The dancing had been going on quite a while before we arrived. The costumes lived up to anything ever conjured up in my childhood imagination. The men wore great head-dresses of eagle feathers, and their faces were painted, their bodies too. The dancing seemed simple on first view, but appeared to be more and more difficult as we watched. The rhythms were very intricate, not the simple repetition of the same beat that we are accustomed to in our "Western" music, but it seemed to me that the beat changed frequently (i.e., from 3/4 to 5/4 to 2/4, etc.). The dance was solemn, and the rhythm of the tom-toms and the chant of the singers were punctuated at times by war whoops of the dancing men. I blush to add that our Bobby was quite carried away by it all and finally joined lustily in the war whoops.

We returned from the pueblo around five and then entertained real, live company right smack in the middle of all our worldly goods. (I had borrowed a hot plate the night before, did the cooking and simply warmed dinner on our "black beauty" upon our return.) A slightly limp cactus graced the table as centerpiece, and two dish towels subbed for a tablecloth. Our menu was expedient; I can't think of anything else to call it. I had a veal roast, but the thought of attempting to roast it in my miserable oven was too depressing. So, I jammed it into the pressure cooker and it came out looking as though it would much rather have been roasted.

Our guests were two completely balmy SEDs, Bob and Norman. Bob, an attractive fellow with a nice smile, was in high spirits. He told us that next Wednesday he is going to fall madly in love with a girl named Shirley. A whirlwind romance will follow, culminating in marriage sometime in December. I was most impressed, but a little baffled by it all. But there is an explanation. Military regulations here

forbid the wife of an enlisted man to come to live at Sh-La.
If Bob goes home to marry his Shirley, he'll have to leave
her and return to our little exile alone. However, if Shirley
qualifies for a position here, meets Bob here, falls in love
here, marries here, why then, she can stay. In fact, she has
to stay! Hence the plotted romance. See? And Shirley has
already been hired by the project and will arrive next
Wednesday.

All our happy burbling about the approaching wedding
left Norman a little cold. He shuffled about gloomily. I
think he is lonely, and he's already mourning for the lights
of Broadway. When I chortled gaily about the amazing
cliffs in this area, he mumbled something about the sky-
scraper cliffs on 42nd Street. We asked him if he had
explored any of the incredible canyons around. He answered
with a gruff "no" and added for explanation, "No sidewalks." He does not share our enthusiasm for the magnificent forests around us. "Don't have the kind of limbs
that interest me," he moaned. Hm.

But Norman brought along some magnificent records.
After an hour or so of tilting our old phonograph this way
and that, we got it to work and then had a wonderful
concert. Best of all was the Schubert Trio, in B flat major,
played excellently by Feuerman, Heifetz, and Rubenstein.
So the evening was a definite success. I believe we came
out ahead. In return for a limp and anemic dinner, we had
real entertainment and a free concert. And, with this
exalted evening, our social life is launched!

And launched it was! We made friends quickly and found
a congenial world full of animated, delightful young couples.
We learned that we lived in a community where the average
adult age was twenty-five, and where the leaders of the
project were men in their middle or late thirties. We had no
social services, no jails and supposedly no problems—just
petty inconveniences. In many ways our daily life was, after

all, little different from that which we had experienced on our various college campuses.

This evening we were invited to dinner with friends. It was the sort of evening one learns to expect around these parts. Dinner is eaten in a mad rush. The men dash back to work. The wives do the dishes and chat a while. At ten o'clock the men return jabbering a strange language most nearly identified as "scientese." Tonight was particularly pleasant. We discovered we had many interests in common. In other words, we all are very fond of Mozart and heartily dislike Dewey [Republican presidential candidate].

This afternoon a group of Leon's co-workers dropped in. Apparently, they are very charming and comical as well as very bright and interesting. You'll have to take Lee's word for it. You see, they, too, speak little English, but mostly "scientese." The only conversation directed my way was "Hello" and "Goodbye" and oft-repeated moanings about dreading Thanksgiving dinner at the mess hall. Hint, hint.

That the scientists and SEDs worked feverishly and under great tension was evident. Only after the war ended was I to learn that the fear that Germany was working on a similar project gave impetus to the scientific work on our hill. An additional impetus to their work came from news reaching us from Europe. We were appalled as we heard of the official genocidal orders of Hitler's diabolical "final solution" to the "Jewish problem." Many scientists and SEDs on the hill were Jewish and suffered personal pain, threat, and feelings of absolute helplessness as their families, friends, and unknown millions of co-religionists in Europe were imprisoned, slaughtered and fed to the ovens of the Third Reich.

Yet there were those who hoped, and perhaps believed, that this effort at Shangri-La was technically impossible. In fact, one of the scientists at Los Alamos told my husband,

"Leon, aren't we lucky to be here where nothing we do can possibly hurt anybody?"

Muddy Problems

As I openly confessed at the outset, I was, in the autumn of 1944, a nest-builder, a young wife who wanted only to forget that there was a war going on. And I found myself incongruously comfortable and happy in a very strange and secretive place where, like other wives, I knew nothing about the horrible weapons being created there. And, for the most part, I was content to be ignorant. The distance between the reality of the project and my own ignorance and sense of isolation was made all the more ironic by the beauty of the country surrounding the mesa on which we lived.

The area around our hill, in fact, took on a luster and charm as we made friends with the desert and the piñon pines, savored the clean mountain air, marvelled at the snowy peaks and the sunsets that turned them into pink ice cream cones. Though Leon and I both had been raised in cities, we had come to love the rocks and trails and open spaces of New Mexico. The lazy Rio Grande nurtured an equally lazy, relaxed valley life, and the lilt of spoken Spanish began to sound like musical tones. Square, squatty, pinkish-tan adobe huts dotted the valley. Heavy timber called *vegas* protruded from the flat roofs, and from these beams hung festoons of red chilis drying in the desert sun.

It was always a thrill to visit the different Indian pueblos scattered throughout the valley, to get to know some of the local people, to begin to appreciate their art and philosophy, as well as their festivals. We came to realize that we were surrounded by a rich, intriguing, and very special world. Around us was a lovely area that invited exploration. The specific inconveniences of the "garage" we lived in lost importance as we went on hikes, picnics, and out to dinner with our growing group of friends. Then came November 20, 1944:

Help! What complete bedlam! What thorough chaos! It's so hard to figure out what to do that I'm imitating the sailor on the tropical island in *When We Were Very Young*, and I'm doing nothing at all. We have moved as of this noon!

Now for the horrible details. For the last three days we have had a more or less half-hearted snowfall. Today the weather turned warmer with unquestionably gooey results. Lee came racing home through the slop at 12:15 P.M. with the startling information that we were to move at 1:00 P.M. That was the first we had heard of it. Well, in no time the movers were at our house, movers who didn't speak one word of English. Pleading with them to wait did no good. So while we packed desperately, they slushed busily in and out of the guck, tracking tons of mud with them. They set our furniture right down in the mire and chatted pleasantly to one another in Spanish, to determine in what order to stow our articles on their truck.

That's not all. When the truck was loaded, we raced ahead of the movers to our new home. Lee ran up the steps, opened the door and called to me, "Phyllis, this must be the wrong house; it's completely furnished!" And it was! The furniture was standard GI (in this case GI stands for "government issue") stuff, placed there, as usual, by mistake

Just then the truck arrived. We shouted, "Don't unload." "Wait!" "Stop!" "Help!" The men smiled, said, "Bueno" and went on unloading the furniture into the mud and dragging the stuff through about twenty feet of mire and squeezing it all into this tiny house! With some more cheerful "buenos" they left us with two sets of furniture, one all covered with mud, boxes soaked with guck, and a floor thick with slop. Our couch is on end, our chairs are piled on the GI couch.

I noted that the next day was Sunday, "humorously called the day of rest," and I continued my dismal tale:

The GI furniture was called for yesterday afternoon. It took a bit of doing to get it out from under our own, but it's gone. Leon and I worked until—I don't know when, because Lee's watch stopped. Again this morning, we began scrubbing and I do mean scrubbing. First I used a knife to scrape away all the mud I could. Lee kept moving furniture, supplying clean water, rags and soap. Then we'd trade. By noon, after washing furniture, woodwork, and parts of the walls, Bobby's room was clean. Around noon, Bonnie and Avery came over to offer their sympathy. We met Mary and Jim [Roberts] briefly, and learned that they will be moving across the road from us. A cheerful little boy, Jamie, about Bobby's age, rode on Jim's back.

There was no time that day to continue letter-writing, but on the next day, Monday, I picked up my tale of woe.

Mac [an army sergeant who worked where Leon worked] is here to help get our car out of the mud so that I can use it later. I need more cleaning materials. Last night our heater got temperamental and decided against giving out any heat. Sunday night is no time for a heater to pull a stunt like that. No one was available to fix it. We put Bobby to bed in his snowsuit and under three heavy blankets. Finally, we found a man who thought he could fix the heater. He succeeded at about 11:00 P.M.

Now the jeep has tugged our car out of the muck, and Lee and Mac have left to return to work. A man just came along and tacked an address on our house. He says our garbage can should be along soon. The clothesline will come later. Someday, maybe, we'll be settled. In the meantime,

I scrub. Perhaps we can celebrate Thanksgiving with a clean house, or perhaps not.

The correct time is 11:32 P.M., and I'm sooooooo tired.

Leon's Letter

To my tale of woe regarding moving to our "permanent" housing, Leon appended the following message before mailing it the next morning:

Please forgive my wife for this letter, but she really needs sympathy. It's been the goriest weekend I've ever known. On a happier note, Bobby is unbelievably cute, just sweet and unspoiled like his mother/father (cross out one). Anyhow, the way he's turned out reaffirms my faith in Mother Nature. Who knows when we'll give Mother Nature another chance? Phyllis is sure eager to do so. But, as of today, my draft status, once again, is very muddy.

And muddy it was! Upon our arrival at Sh-La, Leon had been reclassified 1-A by his local draft board back in San Francisco. This made him eligible to be drafted immediately into military service. This was also contrary to the general rule that young men of draft age (18 to 26) who were working in sensitive positions directly related to the military effort were to be deferred. The personnel director on the project appealed his classification, confident that Leon would be deferred to continue the work he was doing. We had shared his confidence. But the appeal was denied. My next letter home was brief and reflected my feelings.

Well, here we are again—you guessed it! Lee has received the induction notice ordering him to report to San Francisco on December 6. We understand that there is a good chance that the induction location will be shifted to

Santa Fe, and this would mean a brief postponement, perhaps until the first of next year. Meanwhile, we just wait around, hoping.

Today I got the warm slacks you sent, Dad. Now, I'm wondering whether or not I should keep them. There is no way of knowing how long I'll be here.

Well, what a cheerful letter! What else can I tell you? Oh, yes, we now have a clothesline, all our very own. It materialized today.

Bobby loves the snow.

Can't think of anything else to say except, good night and love . . .

No "thanks for the slacks" was mentioned in that letter; nothing, just gloom. Our immediate future was in the hands of Leon's omnipotent draft board. Apparently, they didn't consider his work essential. Admittedly, they had been kept in ignorance about the purpose or even the existence of Los Alamos, and thus had a right to their opinions. One consolation was that we were assured that Leon, if drafted, would stay at Los Alamos, don a uniform, become an SED, accept a $50-a-month salary and continue the work that he was doing. We weren't certain what would happen to me. No one had been drafted from Los Alamos, so there was no precedent. We knew no enlisted man could bring his wife to the project, but didn't know the policy in regard to a wife *and baby* already up on the hill. However, it looked as though I would have to leave our mesa home and return to San Francisco.

3. *Friends on the Hill*

T HE FOLLOWING DAY WAS THANKSGIVING, and I wanted to
make it truly festive. We invited four SEDs and our
new neighbors, Mary, Jim and their little son Jamie.
But, how do you prepare a banquet when you haven't even
unpacked and when Bobby won't cooperate?

Thursday morning I was swamped with work. Bobby
was a very poor help. He's learned how to undress himself,
much to my dismay. This morning, when I put him outside,
he toddled happily and nonchalantly around, doing a
gradual striptease as he went and leaving a trail of clothing
and undies in his wake. While I was dressing him for the
third time, and wondering how I would find time to clean
the house and unpack dishes and flatwear, let alone cook
dinner—Apolonia walked in. I was surprised and delighted,
having been told not to expect her on a holiday. Apolonia
apparently decided to come anyway. She seems to feel that
the only holidays worth observing are Indian feast days
and Catholic holidays. Mere American holidays—piffle!

So, together we cleaned and kept Bobby entertained and
clothed. By the time she left at noon I was ready to tackle
making dinner on and in our kerosene stove.
. . . not that the stove isn't fine compared to the little
black beauty I've been struggling with these past weeks.
The principal trouble now is that when things boil over
and dribble down into the kerosene, horrible black smoke
comes curling up, which just about suffocates us, and flames
leap practically to the ceiling. It's very exciting but just a

wee bit unnerving. Somehow, whenever that happens, I
seem to lose interest in cooking for a while. Then, too, the
oven is very tiny. In fact, I had to squash the turkey in
bow-legged, and it was a comical-looking bird when it
finally graced our Thanksgiving table!

But, we all dined royally on the turkey and all the trim-
mings. Bobby stuffed himself as never before. Then we laid
him carefully in bed. As yet, he hasn't exploded!

Our dinner guests, in general, felt Lee won't be drafted,
but the four SEDs happily offered to save him a bunk in
their barracks, to teach him due respect for an officer, and
to give him lessons in writing home while crooked up in a
bunk.

Lee and I are thankful that we had this Thanksgiving
dinner together, but we have that depressing "living on
borrowed time" feeling. Yesterday, Lee brought me your
letter asking what I want for Christmas. I sat down and
bawled. I want *Leon* for Christmas!

Up on our mesa, the weather quickly grew colder. The
snow transformed our drab environs into a place of scenic
beauty. Sometimes we loved it, sometimes it was simply a
nuisance.

Today is lovely. Skies are clear and the snow glistens so
that, without dark glasses, I'm dazzled. The field behind
our house sparkles in the winter sun and, across the valley,
the mountains appear to be topped with fluffy whipped
cream. They look so near that I feel I could almost reach
over, dip my fingers in and lick the delicious stuff. There
really aren't words to describe it. I can only tell you that,
to an ex-sunny Californian, it looks very exciting—like
Christmas cards come to life.

However, there was another side to it:

Bobby is more enthusiastic about the snow than I am. He tramples it under foot, kicks it around, crams great handfuls of it into his mouth. My appreciation of it is more aesthetic. It is lovely in the distance, but a nuisance under foot. For example, the snow under the clothesline (did I tell you, they erected our clothesline on the north side of our house in practically the only spot on the mesa that is never touched by the winter sun?) has turned to ice, and I skid around hopelessly trying to outwit the temperature and get the clothes securely on the line before I freeze. Today, I decided to wear mittens while hanging out the the clothes, congratulated myself "warmly" on my wonderful idea and started out bravely to face my contest with the elements. It didn't work, not at all. I kept pinning my mittened fingers to the line. It took me longer than ever.

You should see the comical wash I drag in from the line! Bobby's diapers are like little boards. His sheets are rimmed with bands of ice, and on the unyielding surfaces of all the clothing are deeply imbedded imprints of clothespins. This rigid heap isn't in the house long, however, before it starts to sag and droop into its more natural condition.

Lee has returned now from a meeting and—gulp—he says to get my hat, coat, mittens, scarf, galoshes and—we're going out in search of—ice cream. Oh, no!

Day-to-day living was an adventure or disaster, depending on how you wanted to look at it. Our houses were paper-thin. Sand sifted through the windows whenever the wind blew. Sudden downpours of rain turned our hill into a sea of mud. Our single, centrally placed oil heater was temperamental. More than once, we spent a winter night in sub-zero temperatures *inside* our little cottage. Our "quiet" was punctuated from time to time by explosions down in the canyons. These explosions were often enough to shake our flimsy houses and set all the pictures on the walls askew. We would straighten the pictures and then, BANG, another explosion and once again, pictures to straighten.

Admittedly, these inconveniences were nothing compared to the work of the project close at hand, and certainly nothing compared to the wars raging overseas. To be honest, I simply tried not to hear the sounds of war in those explosions. Instead, I did my best to master the art of cooking on a primitive stove, and to adapt successfully to the "hardships" of mud, cold, shortages, the isolation from normal society, and accept my ignorance of the work being done on our mesa and in the canyons surrounding it.

Minnie

In all matters, emergency and routine, people were the real lifesavers. We made many wonderful friends at Los Alamos, with whom we shared a lot. Many are still very dear to us today. There were, of course, many famous physicists there— Robert Oppenheimer, Enrico Fermi, Edward Teller, to name a few. (Some real names were not used. By chance I once met Niels Bohr, the eminent Danish physicist, at the commissary. I had occasion to speak to him on the profound subject of ration stamps necessary for the purchase of certain foods. His ration book bore the name Nicholas Baker, not Niels Bohr.) My husband related to some well-known physicists in his work such as Luis Alvarez, who was his supervisor, and Robert Bacher, who was Alvarez' supervisor and, on occasion, Robert Oppenheimer. Occasionally, we met very prestigious scientists at social affairs. But for me, life was largely confined to close friends—friends like Minnie, whose first appearance in our neighborhood shocked me.

We've been living in the only house that has been completed in this corner of the project until now. I've been too busy to be lonely. A house was tossed together right next to ours this week and "finished" yesterday. I've been watching eagerly to see who the occupants will be. Well, I just caught my first glimpse of "her" and now my eagerness has turned to apprehension.

I looked up over my typing and saw the door across the way open very slowly and the saddest-looking creature sort of sagged out. Her hair is a tangled mess; her clothing, all awry. She is long, slim, and right now she is leaning against the porch post, looking vaguely around through bleary eyes. Evidently she doesn't share my enthusiasm for the place. She just glanced over here, may have seen me, and now has dragged herself back into her house, and the door is slowly, s-l-o-w-l-y closing. So, I have a new neighbor!

The following day, I learned why my new neighbor had appeared so bedraggled. The previous day, Minnie had arrived by train at Lamy, the nearest railroad station to Santa Fe. I must add that Lamy was and still is absolutely nothing but a water tower, a bar, and a few scattered adobe huts. Minnie had come to that desolate spot with her two-and-a-half-year-old son Billy. Her husband was driving from the University of Illinois in Urbana to the project, transporting needed equipment to Los Alamos in a trailer (I learned months later that he moved a cyclotron to the project). Minnie was met at Lamy by a GI with a jeep, and was bounced by jeep to the office in Santa Fe. There Minnie was told that she was expected on the hill and that arrangements had been made for her. She was to drive up to Los Alamos with a Frenchman who was also coming for the duration of the war.

They received the same directions we had received, but they became confused as darkness descended on the desert. They took a wrong turn, towards Frijoles Canyon instead of towards Shangri-La and, near some desolate Indian ruins, got stuck in the snow. After trying in vain to get the car out of the snow bank, the Frenchman left Minnie and Billy in the car and wandered off hoping to get some help. He made it back to the valley about midnight, completely hysterical. As far as I know, he never came back to Minnie or to the project. Minnie was left in a drafty, unheated car in a heavy snowstorm. She tried desperately to keep her little son warm and cheerful.

When the expected car with Minnie and the Frenchman failed to show up at the project gate, MPs were dispatched to search all the roads. At about 4:00 A.M., they found Minnie and Billy and took them in an open jeep up and down the mountain roads until they reached our mesa. After hearing her story, my only wonder was that Minnie didn't look worse when I first saw her drooping at her doorway. I liked her at once, and we quickly became good friends.

Minnie was energetic and determined to cope. After a severe dust storm powdered our houses an ashen gray, I was amazed to see my tall, strong new friend carry her furniture outside, clean like mad, and lug it right back inside the house. While in college in Nevada, Minnie had been a forward on a girls' basketball team that had won a state championship. That was more proof to me that Minnie could do absolutely anything and, like the water tower, the tall, cheerful Minnie became a symbol to me of strength and survival.

Margaret

But, there were others, like very pretty, very pregnant, and very helpless Margaret. I called on her soon after she moved across a ditch from my little box of a house and found her in tears. She was exhausted after moving in, having suffered the usual mix-ups. They had been moved into the wrong house, but that was the least of her problems. She couldn't accept the fact that her Harry, like my Leon, worked late many evenings and she had no idea of the work he was doing. She asked. He clammed up. She had found a wall there that never was there before. I felt she was borrowing trouble and I realized she was frightened. She complained about everything, the people, the commissary, the wind and snow. One night, Harry walked out and didn't return until morning and then told her he couldn't stand any more.

I remember trying to tell her she'd have to put up with a lot here. Their briefing before they left for Shangri-La should have been some preparation. I felt she would have to grow up in a hurry; I knew I had to. She would have to find a way to scale the growing wall between them. But Margaret couldn't adapt, needed home and mother desperately, and a few weeks later left our mesa, never to return. Harry moved to the dorm. I felt discouraged. In the weeks before she left, I had tried to introduce her to friends, show her around and generally be a friend, but I hadn't been enough help. Perhaps no one could have been.

Brad and Louise

Just down the road lived what we considered an "older" couple who had a tiny son named Eric. (Older, in our youthful society, meant late thirties or early forties.) Louise, tall and thin, with a birdlike appearance and lively tongue, seemed to know more about what was going on than anyone else in our area. In the early months of our stay at Los Alamos, Louise was more than willing to share her information. For example, she would tell me that things are "really coming to a boil at South Mesa," or "Today's the big day at K Site," and sure enough, there would be sounds of explosions from the area she had indicated. I was impressed. Leon had never given me any hint of the activities at the various sites. This might mean (to me in my ignorance before the war's end) that Louise's husband Brad was privy to more information than Lee was. Thus, I concluded that he was, indeed, an important person on the hill. Brad's behavior substantiated that assumption. Many an evening he would sit on his front steps, puff in a desultory way on a pipe, and gaze solemnly out into space. At such times, Louise would caution all of us not to interrupt him. He was clearly deep in thought. So was I as I watched him.

Little by little, incidents occurred that would shake my faith in "the thinker." Brad, knowing that we were seriously interested in classical music, would question us as to the "definitive" recording of a particular symphony. On his next trip to Santa Fe, he would purchase the record we had recommended. I felt flattered that he would consult us. We learned only later that although he collected records, he had no phonograph on which to play them. Food for thought! One evening he brought a book to our house for Leon to look over. It was a book by an English engineer who devoted pages and pages of print to debunking Einstein's theory of relativity. Generously, Brad told Leon that he could borrow it. Leon politely tried not to take the proffered book. He told Brad that it would be a long time before he would get around to reading it. There was no hurry about returning it, Brad assured him, as he had bought two copies of the book! Still, he sounded important, acted important, and what's more, Louise reinforced my impression of Brad by the deference she showed him.

The Thin Man

The area in which we lived consisted of a small gridiron of square, flat-roofed, prefabricated houses. These were known as the McKee Houses and labeled McKeeville by their little band of residents. Somewhere between McKeeville and Bathtub Row was a wide open terrain that the optimistic among us called "The Field." Although most of the area was completely bare, it contained a swath of stubby grass-like growth

crisscrossed by narrow paths. I went to this locale with
Fawn one windy afternoon.

Fawn had been to the vet's for some sort of problem. I
only remember that the vet assured me that, although he was
still not well, he was not contagious to people; but he *was*
contagious to dogs. Why not, I reasoned, take him over to
the field, away from other animals, and let him run? So,
I carried Fawn over to the field and, once at my destination,
let him loose amid the stubble. My grateful dog, intoxicated
with his freedom, sped around me in huge, joyous circles.
From nowhere, there appeared a little black dog who was
obviously eager to cavort with Fawn. In no time I, too, was
racing around in circles, trying to keep the dogs separated
and alternately trying to grab my speeding canine.

Then I noticed a rather bedraggled, skinny man coming
along one of the crisscrossing paths. He walked quickly and
appeared to be somewhat tilted forward. He wore a nondescript, narrow brimmed hat. As he came down the trail,
I called to him.

"Quick, grab that dog!" pointing to the black one.

"That one?" he asked.

"Yes, quickly!" I directed as the black dog shot by him.
And, with his long, skinny hands, he deftly grabbed the little
fellow.

"What's going on?" he asked.

"Just hang on until I get this one," I shouted breathlessly
while running, indicating as best I could my gyrating fox
terrier whom I finally managed to corral.

"Now wait until I get away," I ordered. Then, briefly, I
explained the problem, adding, "I'm so glad you happened
by."

"I didn't *happen* by!" he declared in an irritated tone, and
then, pointing to a house on Bathtub Row, he added, "*This* is
where I live."

I knew the house to which he was pointing. It was the
home of the project director, Robert Oppenheimer! And so,

therefore, the gaunt man standing before me must be . . . !
Oh dear! He laughed at my sudden embarrassment and, as
he did, I noticed that he had the most amazing lavender-blue
eyes, which made his thin face almost beautiful.

Later, of course, Leon learned about my encounter and
corroborated my conclusion. Yes, from my description that
had to be Oppie. No, that wasn't exactly an ideal way to meet
the project director. Yes, I'd better find another place to
exercise our dog.

After we had discussed the incident of the field, Leon told
me about Oppie's very considerable skill as project director.
Oppie, he said, seemed to know everyone on his huge staff
and to know what everyone was doing. He thoroughly understood many aspects of the work going on and understood it
well. He listened carefully. His span of scientific information
was exceptionally wide. His style of leadership emphasized
open discussion and consensus. At the same time, he was
capable of cutting sarcasm. He had an absolute genius for
ferreting out the mistakes of others. Somehow, his methods
were working excellently and he seemed to be an ideal leader
for his devoted staff on the hill.

This sounded so different from the Professor Oppenheimer
whom I had known by reputation at the university. This was
the man whose courses were fascinating but very difficult,
whose conversation was circumlocutory and almost deliberately obscure. This was the poetic dreamer, the social
reformer, the Sanskrit scholar, as well as the brilliant the-
oretician who held concurrent appointments at both the
University of California at Berkeley and at the California
Institute of Technology at Pasadena. And this also was the
man who, at my insistence, obligingly—well, somewhat
obligingly—held a stray dog while I rounded up my ca-
vorting, disobedient Fawn. So there it was! Deference to
Brad and orders to Oppie. What else was I going to mix up?

Richard

Norman, our dour SED friend, seemed to be clearly displaced from his New York environment. Military procedures were an anathema to him. He coped as best he could, bringing up to the mesa a collection of fine classical records and sharing them with his friends. He was a founder and one of two members of the "Mushroom Society," which indulged in recordings of Gustav Mahler in the evening in the tech area. Lee and I would stand outside the tech area fence (because I couldn't go in), sometimes in the snow, to listen through the opened window to some first-rate music.

One day, Normie told Leon about a talented mathematician who was a friend of his and was about to be drafted. He wondered if it would be possible to get his friend to Los Alamos. Leon conveyed the information to Luis Alvarez; and just two weeks later, news circulated the labs that a new recruit—Norman's friend—was expected to arrive on the hill any day. He was Richard Bellman, a graduate student at Princeton. Without going through basic training, Richard was whisked off to Los Alamos to join the other SEDs. And, for once Normie was positively joyous, even excited.

I was delighted with Richard when I met him. His handsome appearance and boyish grin, his friendly nature and genial wit were a great addition to our mesa life. He had recently married Betty, a WAC, and Betty had succeeded in getting a transfer to Bruns Hospital, a military hospital near Santa Fe.

On meeting Richard, I invited him to our house for dinner. He accepted with alacrity. However, the day he was to come, an MP showed up at my door with a hastily written note from Richard. There was no way that Richard could come for dinner. No way! He was suffering utter misery in the hospital. Would I please come to the window of his hospital room?

At the barracks the "senior" SEDs had warned him of the

stupidity and the pitfalls of living under military rule, but the buoyant Richard would hear none of it. He was determined to look at the good side of his present state of affairs. He had been drafted to do scientific work. That was great! There was his Betty nearby, sheer luck! And since there was free medical care, why not take advantage of it? He was in fine health, but was a little annoyed by some nagging athlete's foot. Why not, he had reasoned, consult a physician and take advantage of what the system had to offer?

Once at our hospital, he was assured by the doctor that his minor condition could be treated very simply. He was sent to a small room. An orderly came in with the appropriate medicine and proceeded to give Richard a foot bath. The orderly had the correct medicine all right. He simply had neglected to read the directions on the bottle and dumped the medicine into the foot bath full strength.

Following Richard's directions, I dragged a box to the appropriate hospital window, climbed up on it and peeked in. There was my new friend, utterly miserable, huddled over with a towel around his shoulders, and soaking his red, raw feet in a tub of solution. His first words were, "They got the athlete's foot all right, but they almost got my feet as well. Does *everything* work like this up here?"

"Not quite everything," I answered. "Once in a while something really works out right." The dinner I had cooked would come to him, we decided, and we'd come with it and serenade him outside his window. Which we did.

Bob's Courtship

As I had said, now and then things went as planned. For example, the two young people, Bob and his Shirley, had found a way around their difficulties and were willing to put up with a very inconvenient living situation in order to be together. On December 7, I could report:

To happier news. You'll be amused to know that Bob's Shirley arrived last week. The whirlwind courtship took place exactly as we knew it would and now we're invited to the wedding. Shirley has a job here as a librarian and has been assigned a room in one of the large dormitories. Bob, a GI, will continue to live in the army barracks. It's not exactly ideal, but they consider themselves lucky. The wedding will be held in a tiny church in Santa Fe, and eight of us will make up the wedding party. There will be a wedding dinner at the plushy (relatively) La Fonda hotel, a place we love.

The wedding went off just fine—with only one hitch. In my report on the festivities, our concern about personal transportation came through.

After a delicious dinner at the La Fonda, we took the newlyweds to the bus station for the trip to Albuquerque where they would spend their weekend honeymoon. Well, the bus came along, crowded to the hilt, and the driver refused to take them. We all looked at one another. Then Lee said, "O.K., hop in, we'll drive you." And we did, all 72 miles of the way! We arrived in Albuquerque about 11:30 P.M. and dropped them off at their hotel, after which Lee insisted on rousing Harold [Shapiro], our closest friend in Albuquerque, for a reunion. [Harold, though a mathematician, taught physics at the University of New Mexico].

A sleepy bunch got together, and it was great fun. But we drove back through the coldest night you can imagine. The trip back took four hours. Now with gas rationing, we'll have none for—who knows how long? Our tires have about had it, too. The roads here are awful, like giant washboards. Our tires were not designed for the kind of workout they're getting.

We've heard that the road to our mesa will soon be

repaired and here's why. Some GIs drove our top Army brass into Santa Fe last week in a carryall that had the springs blocked, purposely of course, with pieces of wood! The big boss man was really sore—and easily convinced that something must be done. Agreed, but when?

Our biggest worry now is where do we look for tires? We know there are none in Shangri-La, so we may be grounded for the duration.

4. *Looking Around*

Dealing with the Outside World

TIRES! WHERE WOULD YOU LOOK? Well, there was Santa Fe only forty miles away. Santa Fe was a tiny, exceedingly picturesque town of tile-roofed, pinkish adobe houses and lovely gardens tucked inside squatty adobe walls. It had a long and colorful history, an identity, and more important, it had bathtubs, water, sufficient electricity, shops, stores and, glory be, even garages! The Santa Feans, proud of their traditions and overflowing with civic pride, were happy with their separateness.

Off the hill and into this little paradise came hoards of shabby oddballs with their dusty kids. To make matters worse, the oddballs had no names and all gave the same address, "Box 1663, Santa Fe." It was apparent that although we gave an address in their town, and all gave the same address, we certainly didn't live in Santa Fe. Moreover, following military orders we were distant, unfriendly and completely noncommunicative. They assumed (they could see lights from our mesa at night) that we were swarming all over the Pajarito Plateau; and when they would ask why we were there, we'd give an answer like, "Oh, we're making windshield wipers for submarines." To add to the annoyance of the Santa Feans (and to us), their town was liberally sprinkled with FBI as well as Army intelligence agents. Clearly these residents bore some of the brunt of the rapid population growth on one of the mesas up on the Pajarito Plateau.

And Santa Fe was swamped with requests from these nonexistent residents of the hill. Products in their stores were rationed, based on the population of Santa Fe alone. No, there were no tires for us in Santa Fe, no new tires, no old tires, no retreads, no recaps, none! So, we used our car as little as possible, drove when we had to on treadless tires—and waited . . .

And waited, for a series of miracles. Caught up in the web of the ubiquitous military presence on our hill, we coped as best we could with many rules that made no sense to us (for example, my experience with Fawn and the "gate"). However, much more important to us was the baffling and completely uncertain status of Leon's draft classification. It seemed to me that Leon's draft board was as determined to get him as Inspector Javert was to get his prey in Victor Hugo's *Les Miserables*. This situation in particular kept us, so to speak, hanging over a cliff like those so common around the mesa. On November 23, Leon's draft record had been transferred to Santa Fe. My husband's immediate superior as well as the personnel officer at the site continued to assure us that they were objecting strenuously and officially. I learned, though, that if they failed, I would be sent home promptly and permanently. There seemed to be no military clause anyone could find that would permit my continued presence on the hill. Things climaxed sooner than we expected, as I recorded in my December 12 letter:

Well, we do have great news here. Guess I should give it to you chronologically. Last Saturday (December 9), Lee received his final notice to report to Santa Fe on Tuesday the 12th for induction. Yes, that's today! Lee took the notice directly to the proper person, the one who had been so reassuring. He read it and then said, quite calmly, he'd see what, if anything, could be done. His attitude seemed so different.

Need I say, we spent one miserable weekend—and I had a nasty cold to boot. Couldn't eat or sleep. Lee was

depressed and remarked sadly that we were all just pawns
on a chessboard and no use pretending we were the
players.

But, after talking to Lee, the officials here really got
busy, and had the wires to Washington steaming. In the
meantime, Lee made plans. The last bus to Santa Fe on
Monday left at 5:00 P.M.

Luis Alvarez, leader of the group in which Lee worked,
asked him, on Monday, to attend a meeting of the group on
Monday evening. Lee responded that he could not attend
because he had to take the bus to Santa Fe and stay in a
hotel overnight so that he could be inducted at 8:00 A.M.
Tuesday morning. Luis asked, "What if I arrange to have
you chauffered in an Army car tomorrow morning at 6:00
A.M.? Would you be willing to stay and attend the meeting?"
Lee said, "Yes." (It probably would have been the first time
in the history of the United States that an inductee would
have been chauffered in an Army car to his induction.)

Finally, a last minute phone call was put through which
brought results. At 4:50 P.M. Monday a "STAY OF
INDUCTION" order came through. The order came
directly from Washington and the assumption is that it
must be honored. I'm too punchy from all this to feel
certain, though Lee does.

Lee had told me, as he left for work this morning, that
if he got his reprieve, the whole group he worked with
wanted to come over and celebrate. I called after him,
"How many?" He shouted back over his shoulder, "Maybe
twenty-five," and was off in a whirl of snow.

Twenty-five? Where will I put them? Anyway, we're
together and here for the duration. Hurrah!

He *did* get the stay of induction; we *did* have a large
group over that night. I *did* manage to crowd them all in our

tiny house somehow, and we feasted sumptuously on brownies and apple cider. Somehow, it took the ritual of celebration to convince me that Leon, Bobby, and I were going to be allowed to stay together on our hill in the midst of a true "Land of Enchantment." ("Land of Enchantment" is the motto of the State of New Mexico and is printed on all automobile license plates.)

A Look at the Past

It was time to settle down. We got the nuisance things out of the way. I made the slacks from Dad fit me somehow (or somewhat) and made a fruitless hunt in Santa Fe for an electric plate, finally resorting to sending a letter home requesting that my parents procure one and send it to us. Maybe an electric oven was waiting to be sold somewhere in San Francisco! That would be even better. In the meantime we set out in earnest to explore more of our delightful area. Characteristically, on these trips of exploration we were accompanied by two or three of our SED friends who had no means of transportation off the mesa. On December 14, we found the winding road where Minnie had been abandoned in a snowstorm, and we found where that road led.

> We're sending you a pamphlet about Frijoles Canyon, but it doesn't do it justice. We had a thrilling ride into a canyon where tribes of Indians lived hundreds of years ago. Some lived in tiny rooms in a large circular pueblo, others in caves in the cliffs bordering the canyon. The caves were back rooms, and small structures for additional living space were made of stone in front of the caves. Remnants of these structures remain. We six (Norman, John and Chuck joined the exploration party) climbed all over the stuff and into what we could. Further up the canyon we found a cave high above the floor of the valley.

This cave is quite isolated and approached only by ladders, long spooky ones. Well, Fawn was along, and we took turns carrying him up the ladders. Coming down was another story. The little dog panicked and became a mass of squirming and writhing fur. The big strong men were afraid to carry him down, soooo I did it.

Carrying Fawn down the long, rough-hewn ladders was not easy, but it was a very small price to pay for the rich experience of that day. Spread before us in the canyon was evidence of a very old culture. Hundreds of years ago, a farming community existed here with its own unique social system and a very developed defense system. The kivas (ceremonial structures partially underground) and the petroglyphs gave evidence of the religious practices and the art of long ago.

But it was the system of defense in that isolated canyon that caught and held my interest. Many had built cave-homes on inaccessible cliffs. These dwellings could be reached by ladders that could be pulled up in case of an enemy attack. The circular ruins on the floor of the valley had no evidence of doorways. One entered from the roof, and again, a ladder was extended to the ground and pulled up when danger threatened.

These Indians had lived in this lovely valley for over three hundred years. Something fearful had happened—and they all had fled. Why? What had happened?

Frijoles Canyon Lodge marked the entrance to Bandelier National Monument, an area of the canyon that had been set aside to preserve its prehistoric and scenic values. The name of the monument honors a Swiss-American anthropologist, Adolph Bandelier, who studied this canyon in the 1880s. The lodge contained a small museum over which several lonely rangers presided. Accustomed to only rare visits until the advent of the scientists on the mesa, the rangers (employees of the National Park Service) at the Lodge were delighted to

talk with us at length. They were eager to answer our
questions and to join us in conjecturing about the fate of the
canyon's early residents. Did an epidemic of disease strike
them? Was it a natural catastrophe? A change in the weather?
Flood? Earthquake? Attack by an enemy tribe?

How strange for us, as the residents of another part of the
Pajarito Plateau, to ask those questions. Where had *we* come
from and *why* were we here? We avoided the rangers' questions on these matters. We wondered what kind of disaster
we were creating on our own mesa, only a few miles away.
Would we too leave our mesa and flee like the ancient Indians when the war was over? Two mysteries intersected as
we talked with the rangers in Frijoles Canyon, framed by the
caves and the ruins of an almost forgotten civilization.

We had also learned from the rangers that the Indians in
the New Mexico pueblo area had a known history which
spanned 2,000 years. The Frijoles period was roughly
between A.D. 1200 and A.D. 1550. This small piece of history
and conjecture made us eager to visit different pueblos and
learn more. An opportunity soon came.

In my excitement about other things, I didn't tell you
of the trip to Taos, a most unusual pueblo. I think it's the
northernmost of the Indian dwellings of this type. We
went with Bonnie and Avery to see the deer dance. It was
spectacular.

My first view of Taos Pueblo was overwhelming. About
55 miles north of Santa Fe and at about 9,000 feet in altitude,
we rounded a bend in the dirt road and gazed in amazement
at two immense jumbles of pink-gold, massed, multistoried,
adobe structures which faced each other on opposite sides of a
river. I saw no stairways but noticed that these upper rooms
like those at Frijoles Canyon were accessible only by ladders.
In front of these masses of cubes that were, in fact, primitive
apartment houses, we saw squatty round adobe ovens for

baking bread. Behind this pueblo rose the snowy peaks of the Sangre de Cristo range, the highest mountains in the state of New Mexico. And this was the spectacular backdrop for the fascinating deer dance we saw on Christmas day.

The deer dance! How can I make you see it? I'll try. First a group of about twenty men formed a circle, facing one man in the center who beat loudly on a tom-tom. There was some chanting and swaying. All dancers and singers were in colorful costumes. First came the men doing an oddly rhythmic step. The men moved aside and two rows of women in heavily beaded dresses, about forty of them in all, took their places. Two other women, even more elaborately dressed, led a group of six clowns into the center between the rows of dancers.

The women did a solemn little dance around the clowns, after which the fun began. The clowns had miniature bows and arrows, and they went through some rather amusing pantomine with them. About forty men now entered wearing deerskins over their bodies. Their heads were covered with deer head-shaped forms from which antlers protruded. These men crouched low using two short sticks to support their weight in front as they moved. The clowns "shot" some of the "deer" and left them in a heap. The clowns now joined the other dancers.

The two "special" women next circled the "fallen deer" and shook their rattles as they danced. This brought the "deer" back to life. More dancing followed. Then the whole group of over one hundred danced over to another area of the pueblo to do the performance again.

During the festivities, the Indians moved to a small church in the pueblo and after a brief service inside brought out a statue of the Virgin Mary and Child, which I recall as a statue of an Indian woman with braids and a typically Indian baby. It reminded me of how we all see our divinities and our

legendary figures only in the light of our own visual and
cultural experience.

A Visit to a Familiar World

Early in January 1945 I heard exciting news concerning
another Bob and Shirley, news which resulted in my returning
to San Francisco for two weeks. My sister Shirley had been
waiting anxiously for news of her boyfriend Bob, who was
serving in the Navy in the Pacific area. It turned out that his
ship was involved in the Leyte campaign and saw a great deal
of action. The damaged ship and her crew headed for San
Francisco, coming into port a few days after New Year's
Day. Fortunately, Bob was uninjured and, best of all, he was
home! Very quickly, plans for their wedding were under way.

Leon immediately requested leave for both of us and succeeded in getting permission only for me to leave the hill.
He seemed to be working longer and longer hours and under
more and more pressure. On Monday nights he hurried home
for a quick dinner and raced back to a meeting of his group.
On Tuesday nights he attended the colloquium for all those
with white badges. Now, so often, on the other nights as
well he would hurry back to the tech area and take an Army
car out to the site where he worked.

I felt concerned for Leon but just a *little*, for I was dis-
tracted by the news from San Francisco. I was thrilled over
Bob's safe return, the impending marriage, and my sister's
happiness. Now my mind was suddenly focused on the outside
world. I realized that Shirley had been living under tensions
far worse than mine. Her Bob had been engaged in a life-and-
death struggle in the Pacific. We only had to worry about
mud, isolation, and petty inconveniences. Fervently I hoped
that the weapon, whatever it was, that was being created at
Shangri-La, would shorten the war and bring all the Bobs
home to their Shirleys—and home to stay!

Packing reminded me of the differences I would encounter back in "civilized" society. After a hunt for stockings (fruitless), and a bout of scraping mud off shoes, I got to work digging out gloves, and putting away mittens and parkas. And as I packed, scraped and dug, I began to think of family and friends I would soon see again, people whose lives and personalities had become so distant to me as we had become more and more engrossed in our isolated lives on our hill.

Before leaving Shangri-La, I took a last trip to the commissary to load up on provisions and to leave some cooked food for Leon (who had never starved yet and who probably would have no trouble surviving my absence). In the commissary, a well-meaning but ineffectual Mr. Gonzales presided apologetically over the limp vegetables shriveling in their bins. He watered them carefully each day, but they never responded to his care. The milk was stored in a small chest next to the vegetable bin, but there was never enough milk to go around. Many items were packed in quantities suitable for Army requirements only. On the shelves were gallon jars of many items such as jello, vanilla pudding, and mustard.

I had learned from Mr. Gonzales, as he bravely did his best for us, that the vegetables had traveled from eastern Texas. They had been sent originally to the Army distribution center at El Paso. From there they traveled by train to Bruns Military Hospital in Santa Fe. Eventually, they were sorted and separated out. Well-aged and decidedly the worse for the mileage traveled, they were loaded on trucks. Finally they spiraled up the road to our mesa and wound up in the care of the hopeful Mr. Gonzales, who stood by as they were unloaded, holding his ever-present watering can.

None of the above made sense to me, for I could see fresh vegetables growing in the valley below us. For some mysterious reason, known only to the military, food for Sh-La could not be purchased locally. I could only interpret this as more evidence that we didn't really exist, or that our existence was *not* to be acknowledged.

So I loaded my cart with this and that, submitted appropriate ration stamps for meat, paid for the lot, and headed home. I spent the afternoon cooking, cleaning and mending. When Leon arrived home he surveyed the culinary preparation, and suggested storing it in the refrigerator for his use in my absence. That done, Bobby and I were invited to be his guests at the mess hall.

And if the commissary hadn't done its job, the mess hall really got me *completely* ready for my reentry into the land of the civilized. We lined up as usual with a group of GIs and several other civilians and picked up our trays. They were made of a tinny metal and usually were somewhat dented and out of shape. There were no dishes at the mess hall. Each tray contained about six indented areas, resembling a monstrous, sectioned dish for a baby giant. As we marched down the line, food was ladled into the appropriate indentation and we arrived, triumphant, at the end with a full meal. However, the ice cream, warmed by the hot meat and gravy, swam gently in its section. The various food temperatures melded promptly into a lukewarm average. A slight tilt and everything slopped over into the wrong section. Dinner eaten, I was ready for San Francisco! (And thousands of GIs, who put up with those meals three times a day, day in, day out, and a great deal more besides, were also ready, I was sure, to head home!)

The train ride with Bobby seemed endless as we passed mile after empty mile of desert in New Mexico and Arizona and wound slowly, it seemed, through the farmlands of California. We were on a train loaded with young men in uniform who were being transported to waiting troop ships and eventual combat action in the Pacific. The dining car was in the center of the long train. In the front cars were packed hundreds of undifferentiated-looking, young GIs who seemed able to sleep in just about any position. In the rear were a few cars for civilians, and those cars were practically empty. Our meals were delayed several hours until the troops were fed. Keeping Bobby plugged with crackers didn't always work, and I had a restless, confused, and over-stimulated tyke on my hands.

My parents met me at the station, Mom eager and animated, Dad humorous and philosophic. There were hugs, questions, and everyone talking at once as they welcomed me and reintroduced themselves to a curious Bobby. I remember thinking that they both looked tired, and I recall that they had the same thoughts about me. But where was Shirley? I learned quickly that Shirley was only partially recovered from pneumonia and had to stay indoors and in bed a good deal of the time. Her Bob, exhausted from the ordeal in the Pacific, was resting at his parents' home. Plans were going ahead, anyway, for the wedding scheduled for a week hence. The couple would then travel to Philadelphia, on the east coast where Bob was to be stationed while awaiting orders to return to his reconditioned ship. And then?

As we chatted during the drive home, I was only half listening. I was dazzled by the views from the hills of clean white buildings, the sparkling bay, two magnificent bridges, and the hills of Marin and Berkeley beyond. I inhaled the tangy, fresh sea air. I heard the jangling yet melodic cacaphony of sirens, fog horns, and cable cars. But while feeling bombarded by the sights and sounds of San Francisco, my mind was also on Shirley and her Bob and on the masses of GIs who had arrived with me and now were being loaded like cattle on ships in our harbor, onto ships that would take them into combat from which many would never return.

Bobby couldn't ask questions fast enough. "Where Tan Frisco?" Right here, honey. "Wazzat?" A stop light. "Wazzat?" A police car. "Wazzat?" The bay, the bridge, a fog horn, a cable car, an apartment house, stairs, a whole flight of them, an elevator, a door bell, and, wonder of wonders, a BATHTUB!

What an experience, after the isolation of Shangri-La, to be back amidst the warmth of family and old friends! Conversations were animated as I renewed relationships with all the dear people I had left behind. Was it only a year ago? There were endless questions, some of which I couldn't answer. I had my questions, too, and lost little time catching up on all the news, both good and bad.

I found Shirley delightfully happy although weak from her recent illness. Bob was visibly overwrought from all that he had been through. The wedding in our home was to be small and informal. However, it started off a little bit late.

It was Bobby who distinguished himself by causing the delay. We were all ready to go. Shirley, pale yet radiant, was wearing a borrowed wedding dress. (Shirley hadn't had the time or strength to shop.) I was fluttering around trying to be helpful. Dad, a little stiff and uncomfortable in his tux, was ready to give the bride away. Mother was greeting the guests. Bobby was, we thought, securely in the care of a well-recommended baby-sitter who had been amply supplied with toys, books, and cookies. All was in readiness when . . .

The girl who had been hired to watch Bobby rushed into the living room where the wedding was about to start. Visibly alarmed, she told us that Bobby had somehow locked himself in the bathroom. Dad and I rushed to the locked bathroom door and heard him having a great time running the bath water. I was fighting a sudden feeling of panic, but Bobby was having a picnic. I was afraid that Bobby would sense my fears. He didn't. In his 21-months-old perspective, *I* had come home for a wedding, but *he* had come to Grandma's for a *bathtub* that now was filling with water! How much water was in that tub? How hot? Could he climb, or fall, in?

First, I tried to talk to him through the door. I did manage to get him to move away from the water and stand by the door. Then I tried to get him to understand that I wanted him to unlock the door, but with no success. The little toddler had no idea what I was talking about. So, desperately, I kept him entertained and sang songs with him through the doorway. Shirley joined me and was singing, too.

Meanwhile, Dad called the fire department. Although it seemed a long time, it was only a few minutes before three huge firemen, complete with axes, marched in through the wedding crowd. I was told to get Bobby away from the door, if I could. I asked him to bang the toilet seat cover, which he did, taking only a little time out to turn the handle. At that moment the firemen bashed in the door, and there was Bobby, sitting on the toilet, one foot in, completely soaked but happy, as he greeted his rescuers with "ello."

Then followed sharp words to the baby-sitter, clean clothes for Bobby, and shortly, a relieved family reassembled with the guests and rabbi. The emergency was over. Bob and Shirley took their places at an impromptu altar. It was a poignant experience for all, as we witnessed the marriage in which Shirley became the bride of a young naval officer who fully expected to be returned to active duty in the Pacific.

All too soon, the couple left for Philadelphia, and I left family, friends, and civilization, and the very important bathtub, to return with Bobby to Leon and to our strange life at Shangri-La.

Cabs, Trains and Garbage Trucks

I returned to Los Alamos by way of Los Angeles. There I visited several friends and stayed overnight with my aunt Amy and my grandmother. The trip "home" was relatively uneventful, but had its anxious moments. So I wrote:

"Be it ever so humble" is kinda true. But, I'll start from the beginning. Gram was darling and so delighted with Bobby. She was charming with him and Bobby responded in his most showoff-ish manner. Bobby entertained her royally by eating things off everyone's plate. He quietly slipped a chicken bone off one plate, mashed potatoes off

another. It wasn't funny to his mommy, but he was encouraged by the laughter of his audience. Gram thinks Bobby
looks very like you, Dad, even to his hair.

Taxi cabs were few and far between in those days. So Amy
ordered a cab far in advance to give me plenty of time to get
to the train with Bobby and luggage in tow.

The train was due to leave at 12 o'clock noon. I started
pestering the cab company at a quarter to ten and every
fifteen minutes after that. By 11:10 I got panicky and
appealed to Amy who ordered the limousine available in
her apartment house to come for me in ten minutes. Bobby
and I waited by ourselves in the lobby of the apartment
house and waited and waited and waited. At 11:27 a *cab*
arrived. I called Amy's apartment from the lobby; her line
was busy. So I dashed with Bobby into the cab leaving Amy
to handle an irate limousine driver. It was lucky I did take
the cab, as I arrived at the station at four minutes to
twelve, checked my stuff and *ran* with Bobby to the train,
which pulled out about a minute after we got on.

The trip back to New Mexico was grand, much better
than [the trip west on] the "California Limited." But I
almost didn't get off at the right station. The porter insisted
that we weren't at Lamy when the train stopped at practically nothing but a water tower. He insisted that they only
took on water here. The next stop, he assured me, was
Lamy. A couple who got on at that stop, however,
approached and informed me that we were sitting in their
seats. As they started to show me their reservations, I
jumped up, grabbed Bobby and fled. It *was* Lamy. The
porter practically threw me, Bobby, and our stuff off the
train.

There at the water tank, surrounded by desert, was
Leon. He clearly looked anxious and worried. He was so

relieved to see me, as I scrambled off with Bobby, just as the train started on its way.

And, what a homecoming! First, we celebrated with lunch and treated ourselves to a mangy ivy plant ($1.00). Then, home to our hill. Lee had written to me that our "grounds" had been greatly messed up. What an understatement! Sewers had been laid along our "land." Rain had fallen, lots of it, and snow had melted. As a result, the place where we park our car is now a miniature swimming pool. Bobby promptly fell into it, which immediately made me feel completely at home.

The house is pretty much of a mess, but nothing a few days of scrubbing and a little help from Apolonia won't fix. There is a pile of ironing a mile high, which I'll tackle tomorrow. But, Mary came over, Louise came over, and then Minnie. All were interested in the wedding pictures (which I had brought back with me). Norman came over just after dinner, and we listened to a few records.

The bog outside our house was a problem. It was virtually impossible to walk to our front door without getting mired in the mud. Protests to the housing office had gotten no results. Lee surveyed the dismal scene and decided to create some sort of dry, safe access to our little mesa home. He collected random lumber here and there and pieced it together as efficiently as possible. Triumphantly, he presented us with a plank walk that zigged here and zagged there. No matter; it was functional. It conducted us safely over our bog and left us mudless at our doorstep, a triumph of expediency if not of architecture. Until . . .

It's snowing outside, as I've never seen it snow before. The air is full of it. It seems to be going in all directions at once. From my window I can see little Billy out in the stuff, all bundled up and struggling to sweep the snow off

his walk as quickly as it gathers. Looks from here to be a
losing fight. Fawn is curled up in his box. Bobby is finally
asleep, after practically turning my hair grey.

I put that rascal to bed thinking, hopefully, that he'd
go to sleep. All was quiet. Finally, I peeked in. I looked in
the bed—no Bobby; looked around the floor—no Bobby.
Then I heard a happy "ello," and there my little one was
behind the curtain standing on the desk. He had climbed
out of bed, onto the dresser and crawled across it. Then he
clambered catty-corner off that onto the desk and then
behind the curtain. Simple when you know how! But, what
will I do about it?

Bonnie and Avery have treated themselves to skis with
all the extras. Bonnie has more or less mastered some of
the fundamentals, so she skied over this morning to demonstrate on a little rise behind our house. Mostly, she landed
in the snow and needed my assistance to get back on her
feet. Fawn joined in the fun and, I swear, he heckled her.
Bonnie finally left, promising she would give me a second
lesson soon.

We wrote you about the muddy condition around our
house due to the laying of sewers. Even our jerry-built
boardwalk hadn't completely solved the problems. Bobby
sidled off now and then into the mud and had to be scooped
out of the goo. I've complained and complained, to housing,
to the military, to everything I can think of. Well, yesterday an innocent little garbage truck wandered into our bog
and couldn't get out. It seemed the total GI and Spanish-
American community was alerted. Drivers came in other
trucks and pushed and pulled. No good. An animated
Spanish conversation, well embroidered with gestures,
followed. Then they waded into our bog and appropriated
the planks of our once proud boardwalk and broke a few
trying to pry them under the sunken wheels. No success.
Finally, with a truck pushing and another pulling, the
garbage was under way. The drivers of the garbage truck

were furious and threatened to report [the condition of the ground] to everyone they could think of. Well, wonderful! Though marooned again, I cheered lustily! *Now*, maybe, we'll get some very badly needed gravel. Maybe *they'll* get results.

Minnie and Bill who lived directly across our puddle had also been protesting ineffectively. But it was the garbage men who finally got some results. A battered, worn dump truck finally approached our swamp. Cautiously backing up, the driver disgorged a load of gravel, rock, dirt and assorted random fill, which joined the forlorn, broken planks in the mire, creating a sort of semi-city dump, semi-moonscape between our house and that of Minnie and Bill. A little rough, we thought, not exactly a landscape job, but *dry*!

The First Americans

The straggling little army of Indian workers continued to appear on our hill daily. Stolid and cautious, they possessed a warmth, sweetness, and kindness that endeared them to all of us. The women, who were working in our homes or in the tech area, were earning money for the first time. With it, they bought groceries in our commissary. Some of the men from the pueblos also worked on the hill, mostly in construction or service capacities, though a few men and women worked in the tech area. A particularly handsome, middle-aged man with long black braids solemnly ladled out food in our cafeteria. We were informed that he was an Indian chief.

While enjoying their entry into our world, it never occurred to us that we were intruders into their world, or that we behaved toward them in a very condescending manner. In fact, it was a while before we knew these gracious people as individuals and as friends and not as curiosities.

For example, early in our residence at Los Alamos we

decided to climb a huge, rocky formation called "Black Mesa." This strange, dark mass rises abruptly from the desert near the base of the road that wound up to our own area. Its color contrasts sharply with the buff, red, and gold rocks of the area. I am amazed, upon rereading the letters in which I described the climb, that I was insensitive to the fact that I had intruded on this mountain sacred to the San Ildefonso Indians living at its base. I showed little awareness of their feelings when I wrote:

Today we had a long and strenuous hike up what is appropriately called "Black Mesa," a huge, dark land mass rising out of the valley. We went with Chuck and John, and really climbed. It was steep [going] up, with loose rock all the way, but very, very worth the climb. At one point, Chuck slipped and skidded a long distance down the side. He climbed back, shaky, but all right. At the top, we found a ceremonial circle made of rocks. In the very center of the circle was a huge boulder unmistakenly shaped like a skull. From the top, in all directions, the view was simply magnificent.

Why were we so inconsiderate as we clambered up the sacred mountain and explored the ceremonial rocks at the top? Did we stop to think that the San Ildefonso Indians had a right to their own holy ground? Did we think of them as individuals with a culture that worked for them? Did we feel any concern for them as we invaded their lives and influenced their mode of living?

And influence it we did, as others had before us. Soon after we hill folk began attending their festivities, the Indians began to hold their ceremonials on Sundays in order to attract larger audiences. As we attended their feasts and dances, we found them drinking Coca Cola and saw them wrapped against the winter cold in bright plaid blankets from Sears or Montgomery Ward.

Gradually we began to realize that the cultural influence

was reciprocal. For example, we bought their pottery; they purchased sets of dishes from our Montgomery Ward catalogues. We learned to make frybread, and they made peanut butter sandwiches. We wore Indian jewelry; they wore jeans. Navajo blankets made their appearance in our mesa homes. They put linoleum on their floors.

We were not the only Anglo influence on pueblo life. The residents of Santa Fe, occasional tourists, and a few wandering anthropologists completed the group that were interested in the Indian arts and festivals. Moreover, the whole world in torment was becoming known to the Indians as the young men of their isolated villages became subject to the military draft.

Gradually they became more than charming curiosities to us. As we bought their bowls, baskets, and belts, and as we attended their feasts, we became aware that life on the hill was affecting pueblo life. We learned that because the women were working and shopping on the mesa, their fields were no longer being cultivated. I wondered how Apolonia's life had been affected by our presence. Every day she worked in our homes on our hill and and then returned to Santa Clara Pueblo with money and sometimes with groceries.

"What does your husband do, Apolonia?" I asked her one morning.

"By custom the men do the hunting," she replied.

There was no need to hunt now, I realized. Then what could be his role?

"Oh, sometimes I give him money. He go to the store. He buy food. It's all right," she assured me.

But I wasn't so sure it was all right. The cultural pattern of the pueblo had altered. Now the wives went away to work, leaving most of the men behind, stripped of their traditional roles as providers. And what was our culture like to Apolonia? She said little, but observed a lot. I'm sure that she thought that, in many ways, we were pretty strange. One morning:

I had left Bobby's toy telephone on the bookcase when Apolonia came in to clean. Dust cloth in hand, she puttered around a while. Then while I was out on the porch, she went to the "phone" and picked up the receiver and said a cautious, low, "Allo?" Getting no answer, she quietly hung up the receiver and went about her work.

Apolonia once told me that she didn't "like the war." She questioned me as to what countries we were fighting and for the life of her, couldn't understand why. Hitler, Mussolini, and Hirohito were all new names to Apolonia, who read no newspapers, had no radio, and had never been further from her pueblo than Santa Fe.

Invited to the pueblo homes for feasts, we came to see other aspects of Indian life. Their rooms were simple and sparsely furnished. In one adobe "apartment," three double beds almost filled the room. The remaining corner held a small table and a few simple chairs. Outside was an adobe beehive-shaped oven being used for baking bread. I didn't see a kitchen. Possibly they cooked communally or over a fire-place. I wasn't sure.

As the party went on and groups of Indians came and went from house to house, I noticed that the children were quietly busy. As they played together, their conversation was mini-mal. There seemed to be no discipline problems. One little toddler got tired and climbed up on one of the beds and quickly fell asleep. A cradle-like structure, suspended from the ceiling, held an infant. A rope connected it to a rocking chair. When the baby cried, grandma sat in the rocking chair. Back and forth she rocked. Simple! It worked beauti-fully. The cradle swung and the baby was quiet.

To us highly verbal Anglos, inter-Indian conversation seemed minimal. A word, a gesture, a facial expression packed a lot of meaning. Friendliness was genuine, and that is what mattered. Slowly we began to empathize with these dignified people and to get a real sense of their style of life.

Out of that grew a real respect, and I think it went both ways.

Our feelings of empathy also led to some serious thought. Curious, wasn't it, that our project had to be kept secret from the Caucasian population of Santa Fe and yet the Indians and Spanish-Americans were bused daily to the project? A secret community was being infiltrated daily, and no one was concerned. Was it because these people could be trusted more than the white population? I don't think so. Was it because they were considered too unimportant to be a security threat? Was it because we hadn't thought about them as people, as individuals? We needed their services to stoke our coal, clean our houses, collect our garbage, and twist wires in the tech area. Wasn't it ironic that an Indian chieftain was ladling out soup and serving steak in our cafeteria?

5. *Pregnant Thoughts*

WINTER PASSED INTO SPRING, 1945. We watched the snow line gradually recede up the peaks of the magnificent Sangre de Cristos. Down in the valley we saw signs of green. The valley itself was already warm and sunny. The arroyos (creek beds) were baked dry. Our gravel-topped quagmire had dried, congealing into a solid, albeit bumpy, area between our house and Minnie's. Things were looking up.

Spreading the News

What's more, we had some exciting news to share with both sets of parents. We stood in line one starry night awaiting our turn at the "outside" telephone. We hoped we could impart our news yet, at the same time, not broadcast it all over the mesa. However, the connection was terrible. We tried not to yell and hoped they heard us. As their voices responded amid static, crackles, and a constant hum, we were assured that they did hear and were delighted, too. To fill in so much that I wanted to say, the next day I wrote:

> After talking to you last night, Lee and I were much too wound up to sleep. We talked until well after midnight, which shouldn't surprise you. I'm sort of betting that you did, too. Right or wrong?
>
> Remember, last time Marge [a childhood friend] and I were pregnant together? Well, this time Minnie and I are.

We think we're due about two weeks apart. At least that is what the doctor thinks.

We might as well have shouted our news all over the mesa last night. Here nothing personal is secret. (Well . . . almost nothing.) As soon as the doctor verified my pregnancy, I was assigned extra help, put on a list for a larger house, etc. In fact, as the doctor left me, Dr. B. passed by in the hall, and the OB, Dr. S., called out happily to him that Dr. B. could expect a new pediatrics case in December. (I think in January.)

I know Dr. B. He is excellent with new babies. The OB is new here but already well liked. Not only that, he isn't too busy as are all doctors out there in civilization. The hospital facilities are surprisingly modern and complete. Besides monthly visits, we go to a series of lectures given by Dr. B. Bobby will enter nursery school sometime in November. He'll go mornings until I go to the hospital. Then he will stay all day for ten days (I'll probably be in the hospital that long) and three weeks after if I want it. When I get home from the hospital, I can have full-time help for one week, half-day for the next week, and then three mornings a week for a month. That ought to be ample.

Millie, who just had her baby, raved about the care she received. (Millie's husband, Larry, works with Lee.) Dr. B. has started a system of "rooming in" whenever the mothers want it. If a mother wants to sleep and her baby is crying, she can ring for the nurse who wheels "Junior" back to the nursery. The mother can give the baby his (her) bottle if mom isn't nursing. When I had Bobby, I felt so sorry for the mothers who weren't nursing and who, as a result, hardly saw their new ones. I think this is a wonderful plan. All the rooms are single rooms, so it will be more restful than at Alta Bates [the hospital in Berkeley where Bobby was born].

Visiting hours are at night only. Only husbands can

visit. These rules (military again) sound grim, but actually just about anyone, anytime, can go to your window and chat. I saw Millie a few times that way. Richie, too.

And, while I'm on the subject—yesterday, as Apolonia was ill, Tonita came instead. She is very tiny, young, and surprisingly worn-looking. She is twenty-eight and the mother of *three* children. Learning of my pregnancy (rather, guessing it because I was feeling nauseous), she advised me, "Kid, you should stand on your head or ride a jeep." I couldn't convince her that I wanted the baby, not after she had had three in as many years! Anyway, she left early yesterday. I'm pretty sure that number four is on the way.

Mine was a wanted pregnancy all right, but it turned out not to be an easy one. The tensions on our hill were rising to a climax during the early months of my pregnancy. My anxieties and uneasy health were reflections of the atmosphere around me. I was both elated and frightened. It was reassuring to learn that a whole group of my friends, in addition to Minnie, were pregnant, too. Fine! Mary, Rhuby Jean, Louise, Minnie, and I would all waddle around the mesa together (Rhuby Jean was the wife of Leslie Seeley, who worked with Leon). It seemed to me that we all were striving to maintain the fiction that somehow life could be normal in that very abnormal setting. Perhaps that was a vain hope.

Rumor had it that our general, concerned by the many pregnancies, had instructed the commanding officer of the post to "do something about it," as a baby boom was clearly under way. Just exactly what did he expect the military command to accomplish? He certainly had some control over the awesome "baby" that the scientists would give birth to in only a few months. But pregnancies? I was very aware of the excitement and tensions around me as that horrifying project was coming closer to fruition. Though content in my pregnancy, I felt even less control over the direction my life was taking.

In the outside world, the spring of 1945 brought both sadness and joy. First, there was the shocking, sudden death of President Roosevelt, our aging, ill leader. He was beginning his fourth term as president. It was frightening to realize that this man, to whom we had entrusted so much, was not to see the completion of his task. As little-known Harry Truman took over the reins of government, we found small comfort in the statements of newscasters that he was "cognizant of his shortcomings."

We learned later that President Roosevelt had never told his vice-president about the existence of the atomic bomb project. Thus, as vice-president, Harry Truman was completely ignorant of the work going on at Los Alamos or at the other sites. Reportedly, Secretary of War Henry L. Stimson took the new president aside and told him about the program. Its budget of over two billion dollars had been hidden. Members of the two houses of Congress had no idea that so much money had been secretly concentrated on this project.

The war in Europe was rapidly drawing to a close. The Soviets, pushing west, met the Americans and British driving eastward at a prearranged location at the Elbe River. In Italy, Mussolini was chased down like a common criminal and literally hung by his heels. Hitler committed suicide in a bunker deep under the rubble of Berlin. Suddenly, the war in the European theater was over.

Meanwhile, in the Pacific the allies were on the offensive, island-hopping almost to the threshold of Japan. The joy and relief over the termination of the war in Europe was countered by anxious talk all over the country in anticipation of the disastrous losses of American lives that would be incurred in an eventual invasion of Japan itself.

On our hill we mourned a dead president and cheered the victory in Europe. Many of us wondered what the effect of the cessation of hostilities in the European theater of war would have on the work going on at our hidden Shangri-La. It was evident immediately, though, that if anything, the scientists

and technicians were working harder than ever as all eyes
turned toward the Pacific.

Coping with Secrecy

The approaching climax to the work of the Los Alamos
scientists was increasingly felt by all. Yet, the super-secrecy
of this near-climax made this period almost unbearable for
those of us who were ignorant of the purpose of the project.
We could sense the hopes and fears that charged the air on
the hill, and yet we were unable to share with our husbands
the sense of mixed elation and horror that they felt. Snugly
content in my pregnancy, I nevertheless felt twinges of apprehension as I wondered what monstrous thing the scientists on
the mesa were about to give birth to.

For all of us, anxious feelings were coming to a boil. Our
isolation allowed no safety valve, no outlet. There were so
many similar people at Los Alamos, all carrying within them
the same anxieties. There was no one to talk to who was
outside the system. There were no extended families, no old
friends, no network that would help defuse the tensions.

If there was concern over the morality of the endeavor, it
had to be kept within the scientific community. Scientists,
accustomed to the open classroom, free discussion, and pure
research, had no previous experience to sustain them in
handling their apprehensions. The usual outlet of sharing
anxieties with one's spouse was unavailable.

Secrecy among family members was a new experience for
us all. Barbed wire, fences, badges, car inspection, and finger-
printing gave constant reminders that this segregation of
personnel had a purpose. Some of the European families were
the most upset, feeling, in their semi-captivity, something
vaguely akin to the concentration camps that they had escaped.
But this was a concentration camp with a difference. We
weren't victims imprisoned by wires, but, protected by barbed

wire, we were developing a weapon that could victimize the outside world, as I was soon to learn. The line between *victim* and *victimizer* was becoming unclear to me.

The military personnel felt increasingly useless. Accustomed to combat conditions, they chafed under the boredom of baby-sitting a bunch of eccentric scientists. They stood guard endlessly, but no one charged up our cliffs. Once a balloon was sighted; once a lost plane flew nearby. (Airplanes were not allowed to fly over the area.) These were very minor diversions, and there was no need for action. Completely isolated from the fighting and dying while delivering mail, running the laundry, or collecting garbage, not one of them had a chance to become a hero.

Technically and professionally, the scientific community felt alarmingly powerful. At the same time, they felt personally helpless and politically impotent. They tended to work long hours, any hours. They were uncooperative in regard to military schedules and rules, which were abhorrent to them. They slept late and were annoyed by the "hup-hup" at 5:30 A.M. as the GIs were put through what seemed to them pointless military drill.

Leon and I tried to ignore the tensions mounting around us. We tried, as did others on the hill, to make the most of each celebration. Bobby's second birthday was scheduled as an *event*. As I wrote:

Well, it's happened. Bobby is two and there is absolutely nothing anyone can do about it. I invited the children in the neighborhood to a party in celebration of the great day, and it was a pretty confusing afternoon. You see, Billy had a birthday party just a few days ago. Bobby was highly impressed, at that time, when Billy received presents and was honored as the group sang (somewhat) "Happy Birthday" to him. So today, when a tiny guest arrived and handed Bobby a present, he promptly turned it over to Billy, who, equally confused, accepted it. Then we sang

"Happy Birthday" and both Bobby and Billy indicated by their facial expressions that the song doubtlessly was intended for Billy. When I tried to straighten it out, both Bobby and Billy burst into tears, so I just let matters be. Billy left with the haul, and Minnie assured me she'd get the gifts back to me gradually and under cover of darkness. Sneaky-like.

Celebrations were good tension relievers. We also tried to ignore the tensions as we planned ahead for our growing family. It was fun, for example, to play around with names for our expected baby. Sometimes, we'd try a silly word as a first name. But, one time it wasn't a bit funny.

At dinner one evening, I asked in a bantering tone, "Well, how about Uranium Fish . . . ?" I never finished "Fisher" because a red-faced, furious Leon was roaring at me, demanding that I *never* use that word again.

"What's wrong?" I asked, startled. "I only said, Ur—," and, blam, his hand was over my mouth.

"Stop that!" he shouted, "You never know when someone is right near this paper house! Someone might hear you. *Never* say that! You've *got* to listen to me!"

His anger alarmed me. I was furious, too. What had happened? I was only playing around with silly names for a baby. I had never heard the word "uranium" mentioned on the hill. What sort of crime had I committed? Why did Leon overreact so? If I couldn't know what was going on, how would I know what *not* to say? What was there to stop me from, inadvertently, saying something that was prohibited? And in my own house?

Later that evening, while Leon was attending the colloquium, I made a decision. After putting Bobby to bed, I looked through Leon's university textbooks. I found one written for first-year physics students that I could follow. I looked up references to uranium. I came across a discussion of the work of Otto Hahn and of Lise Meitner. It wasn't easy reading, but I understood that the absorption of a neutron by a nucleus could lead to splitting the nucleus. The result could be the release of an enormous amount of energy. I read lines like "multiplying chain reaction," which might occur "with enormous explosive power." On our mesa? For the first time, I had some real idea of what was going on in the isolation of Los Alamos. My mind was whirling! I had so many questions. Tonight wouldn't be the time to ask them. How long would I have to wait?

Little lady of Hiroshima, I was terrified as I read that textbook. How dangerous was Leon's work? What if there were an accident here? I knew that the scientists on the hill were fearful of fire, and no wonder! I thought of our chronic water shortage on the mesa. Oh, my God! Could we all be killed here?

My mind kept going back to the word "enormous." Aren't wars bad enough now? Could this weapon wipe out entire troops? Cities? And what about radioactivity? As it is, the scars of war, I reasoned, take a long time to heal. What monstrous horror was being created here?

Could it end the war? Would all the Bobs return to their Shirleys? Could it be the end of us? Would we ever know real peace again? What about the baby growing inside of me? Would he ever be truly safe? I didn't feel I could even tell Leon I had read the information on uranium. Whom could I talk to about all this? No one. Not now!

Mounting Tensions

I wasn't alone in my anxiety. It seemed to me that most of the wives were feeling increasingly anxious about the work going on up on our hill. At times we would discuss different rumors that we had overheard. Maybe they were harnessing power from the sun, one suggested. But what would that mean? We had heard the terms "gadget" and "super gadget" (learning only later that those were the familiar names given by the scientists themselves to the atomic bomb and to the hydrogen bomb). Explosions in the canyons around our mesa were constant reminders that the goal of the project was to create some sort of super-weapon. Still, I did not share my new knowledge of the work on the hill with my friends. I tried mostly to keep my mind on other subjects. I also tried to focus on the amusing happenings in my life as I wrote letters home to my parents.

Saturday morning early, I dumped Bobby at Millie's and took the morning bus down to Santa Fe. I had a few mere errands, nothing important, and planned to meet Lee and another couple [Richard and Betty Bellman] at 6:30 after work. A friend, Jerry [Alvarez], wanted me to buy some flowers in Santa Fe for a friend of hers who is in the Sh-La hospital, and have them sent up right away. Sounded easy. Wasn't. I got the flowers all right, but then found that the last bus had left for the hill. I was staying in Santa Fe for dinner, and the flowers, already drooping, would never survive that long without water.

Well, I hunted up and down the streets of Santa Fe for a familiar face, with no luck. Then I went to the AWVS Service Club [military] and found a fellow there who knew that the chaplain was in town that afternoon to officiate at a wedding. I raced around town from church to church. Finally, I found the wedding and walked self-consciously into the chapel. There were only the chaplain, bride and groom (total strangers to me), and six others. I felt distinctly out of place. The wedding over, I went up, congratulated the bride, who looked blank but happy and who reached out vaguely for the flowers. I hung on to the flowers and started to speak to the chaplain when I suddenly got a nosebleed, turned, and fled. I ran into a room by the chapel and watched for the chaplain to emerge.

When he did, I called to him. Thinking I was crying, he
put a consoling hand on my shoulder and asked if he could
assist me in any way! Yes, a handkerchief! Which he
produced! Then I told him the problems of my floral mission, he agreed to take the flowers back to the hospital for
me, and the day was saved!

That same day, after work, Lee picked up Bobby and also
Bob and Shirley, who were heading off on a brief vacation.
He left the couple at a bus stop, and then he and Bobby
joined me at the La Fonda in Santa Fe. Soon Dick was on the
scene, proudly introducing us to his Betty, who had arrived
recently and had started her nursing duties at Bruns Military
Hospital. Betty seemed lively, vivacious, and high-spirited.
Dinner at the La Fonda was a little hectic. Bobby was
starving and he loaded up with crackers, bread, and anything
he could get his hands on. Dick and Betty kept up an exceedingly animated conversation, often both talking at once. The
food was hot and spicy and a great change from Los Alamos
fare.

After dinner, I took Bobby to the bathroom and, to my
surprise, met Alice Hoyt whom I had known when she was
dean of women at the University of California at Berkeley
back in my student days. Those carefree days suddenly seemed
to have been ages ago. She was equally surprised to see me.

"Are you here on a vacation?" she asked.

"No," I replied vaguely (or evasively), "we are living
nearby for a while."

She wanted to know more. Did I have a phone number?
Could she reach me? Could we get together sometime? But
quickly she seemed to sense that she shouldn't ask questions.
Much as I would have liked to, I didn't see her again.

The following letter describes the rest of that day:

Soon we were on our way back. Bobby went to sleep in
the car. Fawn curled up next to him, and both ignored the

lively conversation. It was no problem entering Bruns Hospital grounds to leave Betty off. Leaving wasn't as simple. We stopped at the pass gate there, and a very, very drunk sentry got friendly with Leon. When we started to drive out of the hospital grounds, he ordered us to back up and turn off our car lights. We didn't like that a bit, but obeyed. After all, drunk or sober, he was an armed sentry. The MP shoved a whiskey flask towards Leon and grandly offered a "great guy" a drink. Lee didn't think he needed one, but pretended he did. It was a while before we could extricate ourselves from our newly found "friend," but soon we were on our way, feeling it had been quite a day. However, we weren't through.

Out on the so-called highway a patrol officer in a police car signalled us to pull over. We were dumbfounded! It was past midnight. We were not driving fast. There wasn't another car for miles around. This was the first patrol car we had ever ever seen in the area!

"What's the big idea?" he barked as he wrote out a tag, "You've got last year's license on your car."

He was right. We had been issued new license plates, which were even now in the trunk of our car. At Shangri-La we were careless about such things, as we ventured out into civilization so infrequently. Lee showed the license to the officer after extricating it from our trunk. No good. He must return to Santa Fe Tuesday to appear in court.

Little wonder that the license had seemed so unimportant to us. With roads like washboards and no repair garages for civilians on our hill, it was amazing that the cars of Shangri-La residents were functioning at all. Some were wheezing badly. Some died quietly on the hill. Automobiles that were still operating had lost any luster they originally possessed. All the cars assumed a neutral dun color as they alternately sloshed through the mud or jerked over rocks. Clearly, these cars weren't made for the "two-lane highways" of rural New

Mexico. These "lanes" were each about the width of a tire, little more. Rocks and debris between the "lanes" regularly hit the underbelly of the struggling cars. Up to this point, our little wonder had proven equal to the challenge. True, its tires had worn thin, but its tough little motor kept going. Under these conditions, replacing mud-spattered license plates seemed trivial as we hoped that the car itself would survive just a little bit longer. Which leads to my letter of June 7:

Tuesday has come and gone. Lee kept his appointment with the judge in Santa Fe, but the judge didn't keep his appointment with Lee. I mean, the judge wasn't where we had been told to expect him to be. We had been directed to his home. Seems he sometimes operates from there, but no, not this time. It developed he had scheduled another hearing in the courthouse where we finally found him.

He proved to be a nice, gentle, old man, though perhaps somewhat senile. He was apologetic about having to impose the minimum fine of nine dollars. He told us we should feel good about the fact that half the fee would go to the school department, which urgently needed the money. Somehow, we felt no better. We had had a long, hot, rough trip into Santa Fe. Nine dollars is a big bite of money that we would rather spend on our little Hoo [expected baby]. Anyhow, we paid it.

Lee's business with the judge didn't take long. Before heading back we found a nice picnic grove with a lively stream. It was a delightful spot. We enjoyed a bring-along lunch and let Bobby drift leaves downstream. Just as we were leaving Santa Fe, we had a flat tire. We left the tire to be repaired and window-shopped while we waited. Lee dashed into the street a few times to warn drivers of Shangri-La cars to replace obsolete licenses. I didn't exactly approve. After all, which comes first, loyalty to friends, sympathy for the Santa Fe School Department, or Lee's safety?

However, we learned from a bored, tired garage mechanic, that the repair of the tire would be delayed until the next day. There was nothing to do but drive home on our fragile spare tire. Miles and miles of rough road were traversed and, sure enough, poof—another flat tire, and this time no spare. We waited and waited for a car to come along to carry the word somewhere that we needed help. None came, and so we drove the last four miles home on the flat tire. Now it's in shreds. We have no spare. And somewhere down in Santa Fe, our treadless tire is being patched up, we hope.

Leon's phone call the next morning to the Santa Fe garage brought little comfort. Our tire was ready and would be sent to our Santa Fe office at 109 East Palace Avenue and then sent up on the next bus, but there were no tires of any kind to be had in Santa Fe. A new tire was out of the question, anyway. All available rubber and all appropriate synthetics had long ago been diverted to the war effort. And the sympathetic but helpless garage man told Lee that he hadn't seen a tire good enough to retread for some time. So, we were grounded until my father, in San Francisco, could send us a usable spare tire.

At the time, I was deluging my parents with requests for the tire and for other things as well (maternity clothes, baby clothes). Similarly, my parents were making their own requests. They were asking repeatedly if we could come home for a vacation or, at least, a short visit. I got nowhere discussing it with an uncooperative Leon. It seemed out of character for him, but he would not ask Luis Alaverez about a vacation, and he got very angry when I pushed for an answer.

His behavior didn't add to my sense of security as a short spring quickly gave way to summer. Hot dry winds raised gusts of sand that swept across our bare mesa and into our poorly insulated houses. Leon was working almost every night. VE Day (Victory in Europe) had come and gone. Our elation and relief over the termination of hostilities were mixed with horror as we learned of the millions of innocent people, mostly Jews, who had been slaughtered in the Nazi concentration camps.

Staff, both civilian and military, occasionally left the hill for a short period of time for technical reasons. One afternoon earlier in the year, I had returned from the commissary and was surprised to hear laughter coming from our bedroom. I heard an animated conversation and recognized the voices of Leon and Norman. I dumped my bag of limp vegetables and undersized, overripe fruit in the kitchen and hurried to see what they were up to. Lee was sitting on the bed and laughing at the sight before him. Clothing was strewn all over the room. Norman, right before my eyes, was turning from the SED I had known into a civilian. He had on an open-necked sport shirt and corduroy pants, and was busy trying on one of Lee's sport jackets. Nothing fitted quite right and Normie also was laughing. This all seemed quite unusual.

"What's going on?" I asked.

"Norm is leaving the hill for a while," Lee told me and added, "One of these days you'll hear the whole story." Obviously, I wasn't going to hear it then.

"Where I'm going, I need to look like a civilian," Norman added completely unnecessarily. It was apparent that he had already borrowed articles of clothing from others and that he was about to leave for somewhere.

I was laughing, too. There was Norman modeling Lee's tweed jacket, which had been hanging on a hanger for ages. Lee never wore it on the mesa. It was old and limp and bagged at the elbows. Besides, Norman was not as tall as Lee, but heavier, and so the jacket was a poor fit for the masquerading SED. In this outfit he looked a little like an oversized Charlie Chaplin in a tight ill-fitted jacket and loose pants. Still, we thought he'd pass as a civilian. (I learned later that Norman, at that time, was sent to Los Angeles to expedite the procurement of detonator parts.)

The ludicrous scene before me, that day, brought to my mind a line from a ridiculous skit performed in graduate school a couple of years previously. In the skit, a psychotic man with a split personality says to his psychiatrist as he leaves the office, "And, if I return in my absence, please detain me until I get back." The scene Leon and Norman were presenting seemed every bit as crazy. I couldn't make any sense out of Norman's going off anywhere disguised as a civilian. It wasn't even close to Halloween! What nice, comic relief, I thought, for the tensions we all were feeling.

On our hill the scientists were racing around and some were dashing off to an unknown, unnamed desert location to the south. The gusty, changeable winds seemed to mimic their behavior. Mounting tensions permeated the town as high-strung scientists became increasingly irritable. MPs, too, were leaving for an undesignated location somewhere to the south. Rumors spread. Personnel were being innoculated for tropical diseases. Where were they going? And when? It was generally felt by all that the work of the project was coming to fruition. Soon!

As the desert below heated, so did our tempers. July brought its own weather pattern. A bright, clear, blue sky would suddenly give way to black clouds, violent thunderstorms, and sudden, brief downpours. And this electrified atmosphere mirrored our feelings on the mesa as petty grievances were magnified.

What were the petty irritations? First of all, the growing population at the site was using up all the water supply, which, always inadequate, was now becoming critically low. Then too, milk, transported to the mesa in unrefrigerated trucks, arrived in limited quantities at irregular periods and was often sour as well. Little comfort was found in the reassurances by our doctors that milk is sour anyway by the time it hits your stomach; what we got was undrinkable. The hospital, always understaffed for the size of our town, was swamped by the baby boom and by endless demands for relief of nervous complaints, yet it did its best to meet the needs of our burgeoning and increasingly neurotic community. Reports of material stolen from the tech area led to searches of cars. We interpreted this as another infringement on our freedom. (It turned out that the searches were very necessary. Uranium had been stolen, as well as some technical equipment.)

Some of us were irritated, in addition, by a new project on the hill. The nonmilitary demeanor of the SEDs had, apparently, led the commanding officers to order the construction of a rifle range to be used to train the SEDs in soldierly skills. To most of us, it seemed a stupid exercise in futility. Why train lab researchers to shoot? What a waste of time and skill at a time when everyone's patience was wearing thin. And the SEDs, once at the rifle range, lived up to expectations. They seemed to be shooting at random in every direction but at the targets. Children were picking up spent shells all over the grounds surrounding the range. Concerned moms protested at the town council and to the military command, but with no success. It looked as though the rifle range was there to stay until one fortuitous, glorious day when a fire burned it completely to the ground. It was never rebuilt.

Ben, another of our SED friends, seemed to be outracing the wind that was sweeping the mesa and fanning growing tensions. Norman wasn't the only SED who had to be transformed into a civilian. Ben, too, like Norman earlier, was officially required, for reasons unknown to me, to don a similar masquerade. Moreover, he had to make the transformation speedily. Ben, therefore, was given money and sent to Santa Fe on a whirlwind shopping trip to purchase clothing. He returned trimphantly with a jacket, a couple of pair of pants, and several colorful sport shirts.

All assembled in his new clothing, he certainly looked like a civilian (or would as soon as his typically GI haircut grew out). There was just one little problem. His disguise was complete down to, but not including his muddy, regulation GI shoes. When we last saw him, he was racing to the security office to get the necessary permit to remedy that little oversight.

6.   *The Climax*

Trinity

THE APPROACHING CLIMAX to the work of the scientists
was drawing near. Carried along by the challenge of
their work and by sheer momentum, their thoughts
were focused on the job at hand. As I recall, there was little
talk among the scientists one way or the other about the
ethics or morality of their endeavor. The sheer size and
challenge of the scientific effort occupied their thoughts
completely.

I had gained some fragmentary knowledge of this endeavor
on the evening that I had enraged Lee by jokingly suggesting
"Uranium Fisher" as a name for our expected baby. But that
knowledge only added to my own anxiety. Constant nausea
plagued my early pregnancy. I'm sure it was at least partly
due to the apprehension I was feeling.

On July 15, the rumor factory on our hill was abuzz with
predictions of "This is it." On July 16, some of my ignorance
was dispelled. On that date, near Alamogordo, New Mexico,
in a deserted area appropriately called Journada del Muerto
("journey of death") the first atomic device was detonated.
The test was given the code name Trinity. Some of the Los
Alamos scientists had traveled to Alamogordo to set up the
device and to witness the awesome results. Many more went
camping in the Sandia Mountains, east of Albuquerque. They
picked sites with unobstructed views to the south and planned
to stay up all night in hopes that they could witness the
expected explosion.

Leon had no desire to watch the spectacle. The night of the

"Trinity" explosion at Alamogordo, he took Bobby and me camping in the opposite direction from the anticipated detonation. We found a lovely spot near a stream in the Sangre de Cristo range, spread out our sleeping bags, enjoyed a chicken dinner, and settled down for the night. That is, two of us did. But a restless Leon, awake most of the night, was so tired the next morning that he didn't want to get out of his sleeping bag.

I was up early in the sparkling sunshine. I gathered some wood, made a fire, and started breakfast. Bobby played happily, collecting wood (and rocks) for the fire, while an exhausted Leon slept. Finally, Bobby crawled into Leon's sleeping bag with him and took a brief nap.

We returned to Los Alamos in mid-morning roughly at the time the campers in the Sandias were straggling back to the hill. They had seen a brilliant white light in the sky to the south, which evidenced the success of the project! They were ecstatic!

It was then that Leon told me that he had been alarmed by opinions expressed by some scientists during the months of preparation for Trinity. No one knew how massive the detonation would be. Estimates on the outcome varied widely. Emergency military plans had been made to evacuate part or even all of New Mexico in the event that the detonation or the radioactive fallout was much more widespread than expected. Some eminent scientists had even suggested that there was a possibility that a chain reaction would be set up in the atmosphere and that the atmosphere itself might ignite. That of course would have been the end of everything for everyone. Leon had been given the opportunity to travel to Alamogordo for the detonation, but had declined. His partial, but completely illogical, solution was not only to keep me in ignorance of the dangers, but to drive us north in our car in the opposite direction from the detonation. Leon told me later that, as he went to sleep, he wondered if the device would fail completely or if, on the other hand, it might be so successful that we wouldn't wake up at all. Little wonder he had had trouble sleeping!

Later in the day, those who had witnessed the detonation at Alamogordo returned exhausted and drained. They could hold in their feelings no longer and began to speak of their experience. It was as though a dam had burst. Fever-pitch excitement held sway on our hill, as people went wild with the release of long-suppressed emotions. Suddenly, everyone was talking to everyone. In our thrilled, hysterical town there were hugs, congratulations, tears, and laughter. Reportedly, General Groves had ordered that the test and its results be kept secret, but that was plainly impossible.

The "gadget," as the atomic bomb was called, had worked! An enormous crater had been dug out of the sand, and the sand itself had fused into glass-like rock. The crater was over twelve hundred feet in diameter. The fantastic scene at the test site was described over and over again. Newspapers that very day carried reports of a huge "munitions dump explosion" in the southern part of the state, obviously a planted story. But the white light and the churning mushroom cloud were clearly described by the press. There was no way that those of us so intimately involved with the birth of this monster could be forbidden to talk about it. Impromptu parades formed as an exuberant town celebrated the success of the endeavor and the promise, as a result, that the dreadful war would soon be over.

It seemed that almost immediately the jubilation was mixed with profound concern. Sober thoughts circulated on the hill. The monster had been unleashed and there was no way to put it back in its casing, no way to undo the deed perpetrated in the New Mexico desert. The "gadget" developed at our laboratories had power beyond our imagination. It had vaporized the tower from which it had been suspended. It had fused sand into glass. The area for some distance around was contaminated by radioactivity.

Oppie had told some colleagues in the southern desert that

the enormous detonation had brought to his mind the following lines from the Bhagavad Gita:

"If the radiance of a thousand suns
Were to burst at once into the sky,
That would be like the splendor of the Mighty One—
I am become Death, the shatterer of worlds."

The significance of the detonation began to permeate the
hill, and depression and anxiety replaced much of the initially
thrilled reaction. Somber thoughts surfaced through the
joyous predictions of an early end to the war. Many tried to
contemplate the future of a world in which atomic bombs
would be a reality.

It was at this time that I overheard a comment concerning
the possible destructive capability of a hydrogen bomb. It was
the first and only time I had overheard any technical classified
information at all. What I heard was, "I don't believe there is
any limit to the size of the destructive swath. For instance, it
could wipe out all life, burn everything to a crisp within
a radius of fifty miles."

"Is that possible?" I asked Leon.

"Yes it is," he replied, and his face was grim.

"Then one bomb dropped over San Francisco Bay could
wipe out eight or nine counties?" I had a sudden mental
picture of a huge explosion scooping out all the water of
San Francisco Bay, burning all the lands surrounding the bay,
radioactive rain, and, and—

"Look, don't panic," Leon admonished. "This is a theoretical possibility. I'm really sorry that you heard that."

"Have you been living with all these horrors in your mind
for a long time?" I asked.

"Yes, that and a lot more," he replied.

"Oh, honey," I started, "this is becoming an insane
world. . . ."

But Leon wanted to talk no further. There was little sleep

for either of us in the nights that followed as July gave way
to August.

The Mushroom Cloud

For many of us on our hill, August 6, 1945, started off like
any other day. A dazzling sun in a clear sky and a soft, warm
breeze from the desert below gave little indication of the
sudden thunderstorm that was to gather in the afternoon.
Our scientific-military population started to work very early,
as they usually did. The wives and the children on the hill,
used to coping with the now-sandy, now-muddy temporary
environment, went about their usual activities. However, it
wasn't to be a typical day.

We all had a sense that something was about to happen—
but when? Where? The Trinity test, just a few weeks previously, had given us a brief feeling of elation and achievement but, in the weeks that followed, gloom and depression
had returned to our little fortress. Several of our friends had
left for Tinian, an island unknown to us, somewhere in the
vast Pacific Ocean. We had said a brief "goodbye" to Luis
Alvarez, Larry Johnston, Ben Bederson, and others.

On that morning of August 6, my husband left early for
work, and I set about getting our home and two-year-old
Bobby ready for the day, while trying to ignore the nagging
nausea that was continuing into the fourth month of my
pregnancy. But, this was to be the day after which life for us
and life on planet Earth would never be quite the same. Our
turned-inward year was about to end. The isolation that had
led me to call our temporary home "Shangri-La," and the
secrecy with which we had learned to live, were about to
vaporize. On that day, I started my letter to my parents with:

Please note————LOS ALAMOS, NEW MEXICO
Monday, August 6, 1945

Well, today's news makes everything else seem pretty unimportant! You can't possibily imagine how strange it is to turn on the radio and hear the outside world talking about *us* today! After all the extreme secrecy, it seems positively unreal to hear stories about the bomb, the site, and everything.

Mary called to me from across the road. "Turn on the radio," she instructed, "the news is amazing. Maybe the war is over. Maybe we all can go home!" I did turn on the radio and I couldn't believe what I heard.

The "gadget" worked better (!) than anyone dared to expect, and Hiroshima, a city we have never heard of, and its population of 350,000 has been wiped out. The radio announcers could hardly control their voices. They told the whole story. How had they gotten the information so quickly? They named names! Who had told them? They described our hill, *our hill.* They located us on a barren plateau in the mountains north and west of Santa Fe.

They identified us as LOS ALAMOS!

As I recall, Lee dashed home at noon with two colleagues and we tried to eat lunch while listening to the news. Impossible! We were sickened by the description of what actually happened at Hiroshima, but thrilled, too, to learn that the months of tremendous effort had been successful. Stunned by the news, we felt glued to the radio as we listened to one broadcast after another. My letter continued:

We couldn't believe what we heard! 'Over one hundred thousand Japs killed by one bomb,' the announcers bragged. They ticked off the figures as though they were reporting scores at a sporting event. But, hey, those are people! A radius of one mile vaporized, they cheered as I shuddered. They are talking about a populated target, a city. And part

of me keeps saying, "This can't be real." It's also actually
unreal to hear names connected with the project, names
like Oppenheimer, Segrè, Fermi, Bohr and others. After
months of caution and secrecy, it's too much.

Kaltenborn [a news commentator] somehow seemed
more detached and more objective than the others. He took
time, in spite of the hysteria, to consider the bomb's
potential for good or evil. Then he described the first test
atomic explosion in the southern "arid part of the state" in
New Mexico and named the date, the place, and even the
code name, "Trinity."

So now the whole world knew about Trinity! Now I could
explain to my parents a little of my feelings during those last
upsetting weeks. My letter continued to reflect the atmosphere of mixed excitement and horror. As I wrote:

After "Trinity," days went by while we waited to hear
how and when the gadget (maybe I'd better get used to
writing the word "bomb") would be used. Which brings us
up to today. By comparison the excitement on the hill
today has put that of July 16th far down the scale of insane
rejoicing. You can't imagine it. I can't describe it. I'm
certain that it will take time for the emotional bits in all
of us that were triggered by "Trinity" and that blew up
with the bomb to settle down into place.

And so it was that on August 6, 1945, a thrilled but
stunned community learned that their creation, the uranium
bomb, had ushered in the atomic age, a tremendous power
for good or for evil, and with it the realization that mankind
had acquired what nature had not given it—the means to
bring about its own doom on earth.

From the beginning, my feelings were mixed. I was
relieved to hear the joyful news that the war would certainly
be over in a matter of days. But I was also numb as I real-

ized that although the bomb developed at the Los Alamos laboratories would bring the early peace we had all longed for, it had also introduced into the world a new dimension in horror and dread. For these reasons I felt distant from the giddy celebrations around me.

Very soon after the bombing of Hiroshima (why can't I write, "after *we* bombed Hiroshima?"), Oppie quickly raised the question that had been taking uncertain shape in the depths of me. He immediately expressed his great concern for the future of the world unless war could be abolished and atomic power used exclusively for peaceful development. Generalizing from his own feelings of guilt, he would eventually say, "Physicists have known sin."

The Local Newspaper

Late in the afternoon, as storm clouds gathered in the summer sky, many of us converged on the PX. To learn what we could about the outside world's reaction to the new bomb, we were all anxious to get copies of the heretofore belittled *Santa Fe New Mexican*, dated August 6, 1945. This newspaper, usually full of local happenings, cattle sales, small mining disasters, and petty crime, was suddenly our main link to the reaction beyond our parched plateau. In front of the PX, a hot, dusty, excited crowd good-naturedly divided up the few newspapers that had been delivered to the site. These papers circulated from household to household, becoming more limp, worn, and torn with each exchange.

True to its provincialism, the *Santa Fe New Mexican* had two headlines. The first was "Los Alamos Secrets Disclosed by Truman." Obviously, most important to this newspaper was the fact that a local town had been catapulted to fame. The second headline stated, a little inaccurately, "Atomic Bombs Drop on Japan." I guess that sequence of headlines should not have been surprising. For about two years, the

Santa Feans had been witnesses to the smoke and explosions in the mountains to the west and to the strange, secret, silent visitors from the Pajarito Plateau. Now the mystery of this strange community of some 6,000 isolates was suddenly unveiled to them.

There were two lead articles. One was headlined "Utter Destruction Promised in Potsdam Ultimatum Unleashed; Power Equals 2,000 Superforts." This article gave the power of the bomb as greater than 20,000 tons of TNT and continued to state that "It produces more than 2,000 times the blast of the largest bomb ever used before." President Truman was quoted as follows: "It is an atomic bomb. It is a harnessing of the basic power of the universe. The force from which the sun draws its power has been loosed against those who brought war to the Far East." Hiroshima, the article continued, is located on the island of Honshu. Only a few of us knew which island that was, or had ever heard of Hiroshima. The city was described as a weapons center that included a quartermaster depot and large machine tool, weapons, and aircraft plants.

The President also disclosed that 6,000 persons had been working at our site in secrecy on the development of the bomb. "We have spent," he continued, "$2,000,000,000 on the greatest scientific gamble in history—and won!"

A smaller headline conveyed a hopeful tone. "May Be a Tool to End Wars; New Era Seen," it heralded. This article described the initial bomb test in the Alamogordo desert, introduced General Groves and Dr. Oppenheimer, and dubbed the event, "Mankind's successful transition to the new atomic age."

A large article was headlined, "Deadliest Weapons in World's History Made in Santa Fe Vicinity." This article described our town and gave statistics even we had never known. We learned that we had twenty-seven technical buildings, 620 family units, and that two-thirds of us were civilian families, one-third military personnel.

But the most interesting article on the front page began with the exultant headline, "Now They Can Be Told Aloud, Those Stoories [sic] of 'the Hill'." It spoke of the mysterious secrecy involving a group of MPs from our hill who played baseball against the MPs at Bruns Hospital. Our MPs reportedly appeared from nowhere and disappeared to nowhere. Babies, the article continued, apparently were born in Box 1663; people married and died in Box 1663.

Another small article on the front page summed up the dehumanization of war. Four Japanese cities were saturation-bombed on August 6. The fires from these bombings were visible at sea 150 miles away. The reported targeted cities were "Nishinomiya, Maebishi, Saga, and Imbari." All were unknown to us. The same article reported Japanese atrocities against the Chinese. Reportedly, Kweilin, a beautiful city, had been left thoroughly sacked. In Kanhsien, 50,000 Chinese were killed or missing. A thousand civilians were reportedly killed by forced poisoning at Ichang. Death goes on.

More mundane news on the front page (I never saw the rest of the paper) told us that tomato juice was being taken off the rationing list, that Mrs. Giyon had been robbed of money hidden under her pillow, and that a Mr. Chavez faced 100 days in jail for beating up a woman taxi driver. Life goes on.

That the paper was printed in a hurry amid great excitement was evident from the page's layout and plethora of typos. One line I particularly liked was, "Personnel living in dormitories eat. There is also a dining room with waitress services." And I relished that wonderful line, "Those Stoories of the 'Hill'."

We were fascinated as we read about our lives and work and, as we read, we began to find our feeling of isolation fading away. We began to feel a connection once again to the outside world and a need to communicate with families and friends outside our barbed wire.

The Reaction on the Hill

In the days that followed, we waited hopefully for the Japanese surrender that we were sure would come. We knew that our Navy had successfully blockaded Japan and that we had undisputed control of the air. We read of the saturation bombing of Tokyo. After this latest catastrophe, how could that little country continue to wage war? On August 9, 1945, to my horror, a second bomb was dropped, this time over Nagasaki. And so I wrote:

> Now I *am* upset! Yesterday's bombing of Nagasaki was shocking! I cannot understand the necessity for a second bomb. The Japanese were known to be suing for peace and trying to negotiate terms that they could accept. Why destroy another city and its inhabitants? Why couldn't both bombs have been dropped over some unimportant, unpopulated island as a demonstration of what could happen to Japan?

I could only interpret the second bombing as a new dimension in cruelty. We were beginning to hear about lingering radiation from the nuclear bombs and of deaths occurring and anticipated from radiation. Our world would never be the same again. As I shared my thoughts and feelings with Lee, he nodded in agreement and showed me a quotation he had just read in the newspaper. It was by British playwright George Bernard Shaw, who compared the results of this scientific achievement to the accomplishment of "The Sorcerer's Apprentice" (a musical composition by Paul Dukas, concerning a magical power that quickly went dangerously out of control).

Around this time, the military command on the hill relaxed some of the restrictions on persons entering Los Alamos. In fact . . .

I almost fainted when a traveling salesman knocked at my door. There has never been one here before. He had gotten a temporary pass. Amazing! I was so busy questioning him that he had trouble telling me what he had for sale.

Incidents like the above helped demonstrate that our isolation was over and our cocoon-like existence was gone forever. Still, tension on our hill did not abate. One evening, I found Bill Ogle, our next-door neighbor, sitting on the edge of the children's sandbox and saw him shoot a rifle up into the air. To my queries he answered, "I just felt I had to do something." It seemed to me that we all were simultaneously laughing and crying, cheering and mourning. But the war still wasn't over. Was our hope of a speedy end to the war only a delusion? Little wonder that many of us overreacted to trifling incidents.

. . . for instance, yesterday. Scotty, [who works in the tech area and] who lives across the street, called to me at around 9:00 A.M. I went over to his house, found him in bed sobbing convulsively into his pillow. He had turned on his heater, which had exploded and burned about a square inch on his arm and spread soot around the living room. It was just too much and the poor guy was nauseated, dizzy, and completely hysterical. I got him quieted down somewhat, notified his wife, who [also] works in the tech area, and called a doctor.

And my husband reacted in his own way:

Lee goes around with a "Cheshire Cat" grin that won't wipe off. He is very tired and has gotten little sleep. He gets up and wanders around at night when he should be sleeping. And I've lost four pounds in all the excitement.

After three days of nausea, I struggled to the hospital for

medication. The facility was mobbed. Dr. Stout, genial and good-natured in contrast to the high-strung scientists, told me that there had been such a tremendous demand for headache pills, sleeping pills, and medicine for nausea that all supplies already had been dispensed. Replacements had been ordered from Bruns Hospital. Until new supplies arrived, there was nothing.

Disconsolately, I walked home with Bobby. I passed the Service Club. There I watched a mixed group of GIs, Indians, and Spanish workers joining hands and dancing wildly to the tune of "When Johnny Comes Marching Home Again." And the words they sang were:

> "When Johnny comes marching home again, hurrah, hurrah.
> We'll give him a hearty welcome then, hurrah, hurrah.
> For we will shout and we will roar
> And we'll tell Johnny *we* won the war,
> And we'll tell him off when Johnny comes marching home."

Two Mischief Makers

It's not surprising that during this period and in the weeks that followed, I began to have troubles with both Bobby and Fawn. While we were glued to the radio, Bobby, unaccustomed to being ignored, repeatedly wandered outside, undressed completely, and returned to our door. It worked! We looked up startled and there he was—naked again, just as he had been on Thanksgiving Day when he had also been ignored. Then, happy to have our attention once again, he would lead us on a merry treasure hunt to find his clothing. When we went back to the radio, he would undress again. He began to blame his ragged "bunny" for everything that went wrong. Bobby was caught in the act one afternoon at the commissary. He sat amidst opened bags of potato chips, one arm encircling the ever-present bunny and the other busily engaged in stuffing his mouth. He insisted, "Bunny did it!"

One day we gave a young soldier a lift in our car. Bobby turned to him solemnly and cautioned, "Don't wet, soldier." Obviously he was quoting what I had said to him. I had picked this period of tension to toilet-train my son, maybe because I was feeling the need to control someone or something, somehow. As to my problems with our neurotic, little fox terrier, things had been building up to a climax.

I've seen this coming for months. Fawn, fox-terrierishly, barks at all comers. Most people ignore the racket, but not the garbage man. He grabs a stick, dances wildly about acting ferociously, probably because he really feels scared stiff. I've tried and tried to explain, but he speaks about three words of English. Each time we talk, he agrees willingly and most pleasantly, and then gambols and prances around some more while shouting at Fawn.

Finally, it happened; Fawn bit him. He [Fawn] is now in the canine hoosegow being watched for rabies (which he couldn't possibly have, having been innoculated against it). And now we are trying to find wood, wire, and stuff so that we can corral Fawn until the garbage is collected. Of course, a rope would do. Only, the garbage man might make it into a noose. I wouldn't blame him.

Well, the idea was a good one, just hard to bring to fruition. We found wood, purchased chicken wire, collected nails and borrowed a post-hole digger. Lee worked early mornings and late evenings, but it was slow work. The unyielding soil, so muddy in winter, had congealed into solid clay.

"No wonder the Indians build their homes out of this stuff! It must last forever," an exhausted Leon exclaimed.

The clay soil was abundantly peppered with large, immobile rocks. So some of the posts were placed in holes that weren't exactly vertical. This made it a little difficult to wrap the chicken wire around the posts. The resultant enclosure resembled a mouthful of crooked teeth with braces on them. No matter, it served the purpose of incarcerating our two mischief makers. We were pleased with the results. Our "clink" was a practical, if not an aesthetic, success.

One entered it through an "escape hatch" on the outer wall of our bedroom. The opening was about two feet square. Army regulations required two exits to a building. Our little cottages had but one door. The "hatch" was considered an acceptable solution. So, through the "hatch" went Bobby and Fawn, both neatly marooned until rescued. And it solved the Fawn versus garbage man problem for a while.

We congratulated ourselves on solving our own local "war" so easily (although the peace between Fawn and the garbage man didn't last long). We kept as busy as we could while awaiting what we felt certainly must be the end of the war in the Pacific and with it, peace at last. We occupied ourselves with partying on the hill, talking and arguing at length about the use of the bomb, and expressing a lot of petty anger about trivialities. None of this found its place in my letters home. Instead I devoted space to recounting another example of Fisher-do-it-yourself creativity.

You should see the "SS T-shirt." She's some craft, amphibious too! Really impressive. She works with a string. Quite simple. She's a converted carrier, I think. Made in the Fisher Shipyards. She's composed mostly of part of a shippish thing on wheels, a pretty decrepit relic that was a present and had outlived its usefulness. To this contraption, Lee added one post and parts of a torn T-shirt. Now it rides along the land on its own wobbly wheels and gracefully enters the water and glides majestically along to the great delight of our Bobby. We took our creation down to what was the skating rink, now a murky pond, and launched the craft. Success!

Outgoing mail was still censored, although we were told that incoming mail no longer would be subjected to military censorship. However, due to some foul up, none of us seemed to be getting any incoming mail at all during those tense days. No censors, no mail? Hey! What was going on? Still, in the outside world, Los Alamos continued to be front-page news. General Groves was the man of the hour. We residents had known him as the absentee landlord with a gift for saying the wrong thing and for ignoring the basic needs of the growing population on the mesa. For this and many other reasons, the general, long the scapegoat for all our woes and the butt of many of our jokes, was not easily recast, in our minds, into the role of a hero. Now he was honored in the press as the far-sighted planner who was ending the war and saving a million American lives in the process. True, he had selected poetic, enigmatic Dr. Oppenheimer to lead the project. That was either a stroke of pure genius or a stroke of sheer luck. He even seemed to understand the scientists pretty well.

Too suddenly, the residents up on our hill, who were accustomed to fenced-in isolation and virtual nonexistence, were catapulted into the limelight. Overnight, it seemed, news about us was available to all. Information that husbands had not been permitted to tell their wives and that heretofore could not be mentioned to anyone in the outside world, was now being broadcast on the radio and published in detail in the newspapers for all to hear and see. As the scientists were being praised lavishly, many of us gravely wondered if they would someday be condemned.

Little lady of Hiroshima, we were so overwhelmed with the need to cope with our sudden propulsion into notoriety that we had little strength left to deal with the realization of

what the release of atomic energy had done to your two
Japanese cities. While Hiroshima and Nagasaki were in
agony, two thoughts were uppermost in our minds: first, that
we were ending the war, and second, that we now had
reason to dread the future. Some of us tried to ameliorate
that dread by placing a forlorn hope for control of nuclear
weapons in the newly created United Nations. Deep down,
however, I did sense that the sinister shadow of the mushroom clouds that rose over both Hiroshima and Nagasaki
would follow us for the rest of our lives. Not only has it
followed us, but it had led me, more than three decades later,
to your city and to its Peace Park.

The Wall of Silence

In August 1945, as the war was coming to a close, my
emotions stayed at a high pitch. Now excited, now terrified,
I continued to feel alternately close to and distant from the
exuberant cheering around me at Los Alamos. More importantly, I felt closer to Leon. Suddenly, there was no longer
any need for a wall of silence between us. Ahead of us
stretched hours and hours of trying to sift through our
tangled feelings of hope for peace and of despair for the
world.

Night after night we talked. We explored the silence
between us that had affected our lives for a year. We spoke
of the additional loneliness that silence had caused. We
recalled his fury as well as mine on that terrible night when
I had jokingly considered naming our baby "Uranium Fisher."
I learned for the first time the list of words the scientists
were forbidden to mention outside the labs. "Uranium *fission*"
led the list! In fact, the term "uranium" wasn't even mentioned in the tech area or anywhere on the hill, but was
always referred to by the code word "tubealloy."

I learned a little, but just a little, about Leon's research.

His division under Luis Alvarez had worked on the detonation
of the Nagasaki bomb. (Years later, Leon told me that he
was the first to know that the Nagasaki bomb would work
because he monitored the large number of detonators that
were required to go off almost simultaneously, and saw that
they actually did detonate as required and without any
failures.)

Detonators? Suddenly I remembered the box of hollow
cylinders made of brightly colored plastic. They were not
needed at the lab, so Leon had brought them home for
Bobby to play with. They were red and green, as I recall.
Bobby hadn't shown much interest in them. So I appropriated
the small cylinders and, stringing them together, laced them
through evergreen branches and made a colorful ornament
out of them.

Now really curious, I asked, "Were those—?"

"Yes, they were!" he replied before I finished my sentence.

What ironic mixed symbolism! The evergreen branches, a
reminder of life's renewal had been trimmed with detonator
casings, messengers of death! Ignorance had sanctioned that
strange combination. No wonder Leon winced when he saw
the detonator decoration. No longer did I think that Leon
was really unreasonable when he insisted that I take my
creation apart.

After clearing several misunderstandings such as the baby's
name and the use of the detonator casings, we talked about
my lack of information about the project. I wanted to understand the reasons for the burgeoning growth of the hill
population, which always outstripped available housing and
threatened our water and electric supply. Leon explained that
initially it was estimated that only about one hundred scientists would be needed to develop the bombs. Originally, our
community was designed with that number of scientists in
mind. But as the research progressed, the scientists found that
they needed more experts in ballistics, ordnance, explosives,
etc. More experts meant more housing, roads, plumbing,

water, and power, more research facilities, a larger commissary, and a larger military establishment to guard and manage the facility. And so we grew!

I confessed to Leon my fears for the future of civilization and for the safety of our unborn baby. Leon admitted feeling fearful also, but he tried to allay my anxiety. It was important, he felt, that the power and potential of the bomb be known all over the world. That knowledge might be the best hope for peace. Perhaps nuclear weapons could be turned over to the United Nations.

We talked at length about the decision to explode the bomb over a populated target. I could find no justification for it, although Leon supplied some arguments in its defense. First of all, he explained, there was no certainty that the bomb would function properly. A prototype of the Nagasaki bomb had been detonated from a tower at Alamogordo in the test code-named Trinity. The Hiroshima bomb had not been tested. These were different types of bombs. I hadn't known that. The Hiroshima bomb used uranium; the Nagasaki bomb, plutonium.

Furthermore, dropping the bomb over a target, I was informed, was a an entirely different matter than was detonating a prototype suspended from a fixed tower. Had the Japanese been given advance warning, and the bomb failed, no future warnings would have had any meaning at all. It was also feared that, if warned, the Japanese might deliberately move Allied prisoners of war into the target area. An invasion of Japan would have cost us, it was predicted, around one million casualties. Thus, American military strategists may have banked on the psychological effects of surprise and horror to bring the war to an early end and, in so doing, avert the necessity for an invasion of Japan.

As publications became available we pieced together information about the world events preceding the cataclysm of August 6. At the time of the Trinity detonation, President Truman was at Potsdam in conference with Churchill and

Stalin. News of the success of the project was shared with a jubilant Churchill. It was also mentioned to Stalin as a new weapon with unusual destructive force. Stalin reportedly showed only slight interest but recommended that it be used. At Potsdam, Truman issued a warning that, unless the Japanese surrender unconditionally, their army would be destroyed and their homeland devastated. The official Japanese response to the declaration was that it was "unworthy of public notice." And so, Hiroshima was obliterated and only three days later Nagasaki met a similar fate.

Was that sufficient warning? Why wasn't there an alternative, I continued to protest to Leon? Why not conduct an A-bomb demonstration for all the world to see, followed by the deliverance of an ultimatum to Japan? There was no compelling *military* reason to drop the bomb over Hiroshima. The Japanese navy was virtually destroyed. It would take several months to mount an invasion. Why the rush to annihilate a civilian population? I felt it was even harder to justify the Nagasaki bomb.

Was there a political reason for our action? The Soviets, freed from action on their western front, had now turned east in a prearranged strategy known to us. The Nagasaki bomb was dropped two days before the expected Russian offensive, a date that had been officially set. However, Russia had already crossed the border into Japanese-held Manchuria on August 8, 1945, the day before Nagasaki was bombed. Was the bomb intended to beat the Russians before they could grab much eastern territory? Was it a diplomatic victory? Was it the last act of World War II or was it the first act of the "cold war" that was to follow? These were horrifying thoughts for us both. Would there ever be a time of real peace?

7. *Peace at Last*

Hopes and Fears

FINALLY, ON AUGUST 14, came the news of the Japanese
surrender. Suddenly it seemed, there was no war anywhere in the world; no more bombing, no more killing.
Leon turned to me quietly and said, "Now, Phyllis, I think
you can eat." And, I thought, now he can sleep. I continued,
however, to feel like a yoyo, alternating between elation and
depression.

My emotional vacillations were mirrored all over the hill.
There was talk of nothing else. There were those who felt
personally responsible for Hiroshima and Nagasaki. In their
opinion, their work at Los Alamos would produce at the very
least a permanently dangerous future, and at the worst,
global extinction. Some recognized that the physicists now
had a unique opportunity to educate and to lead. They had
made enormous contributions to the war effort. In addition to
the atomic bomb, the physicists had developed radar and the
proximity fuse. Little wonder that they were being lionized
and sought after all over the country. They realized the
opportunity to use their newly won position of influence
might not come again.

There was both a hope and a challenge in the knowledge
that our country was the sole possessor of the atomic bomb.
There was a great difference of opinion as to how we should
deal with our new "possession." Should we share the bomb
through the United Nations? Or should we stockpile bombs
in the hope that our strength would be the best protection
against future wars?

While Leon and I discussed these hopes and fears, our thoughts turned to my sister Shirley and her husband Bob. They were living in Philadelphia where Bob had been awaiting orders to reboard his repaired ship and return to the Pacific theater of war. How wonderful that the need for him to go anywhere but back *home* had evaporated. Now Bob could become a civilian once again, return to California, and get on with his education. So we called them in Philadelphia and we cheered together. Their relief was so evident. And I felt, for a short time, that maybe the bomb wasn't so bad after all.

Now, all the survivors, all the Bobs and their Shirleys could be united, safe and secure, to rebuild their torn lives. The time had come to heal all wounds. The social worker in me sought to respond to needs all over the world. The planner in me saw great promise in the United Nations. Finally, part of me was in tune with the euphoria on our mesa.

Very shortly copies of an excellent little book that became known as the Smyth Report began circulating around the hill. Its full title is *Atomic Energy for Military Purposes*. It was written by Henry D. Smyth, who was then chairman of the physics department at Princeton University. It was designed as an official report to the nation and was undertaken under a directive from Major General Leslie Groves. The first copies of the Smyth Report were issued by the Army. The demand for this information quickly exceeded the supply, and Princeton University undertook to put out an edition as a public service.

Written in terms understandable to a nonprofessional but educated audience, it covered the developments in nuclear physics up to 1940, then told the story of the amazing secret teamwork that had produced the bombs which ended the war. Fortunately for the reading public, the book also describes the reactions of observers at Alamogordo to the stupendous and terrifying test detonation. The summary (pp. 232–233), which was written before the bomb was used as a weapon in Japan, describes the weapon as unprecedented and "potentially destructive beyond the wildest nightmares of the imagination; a weapon so ideally suited to sudden un-announced attack that a country's major cities might be destroyed overnight by an ostensibly friendly power." Dr. Smyth continues: "This weapon has been created not by the devilish inspiration of some warped genius but by the arduous labor of thousands of normal men and women working for the safety of their country." He closed with the hope that readers would carefully consider the ultimate implications of production of atomic bombs.

On our hill, the Smyth Report was read carefully by many residents. I found it informative and reassuring, and was delighted to find that the Army had the foresight to have all this information ready at the earliest possible date. The presentation was thoughtful, factual and thoroughly realistic. However, some scientists on the hill were seriously concerned because it contained material that, in their opinions, should still be classified.

The war had ended. The soldiers were going home. The information about the bomb was available to all who wanted to learn. Still, on our hill, the euphoria didn't last long. On August 21, one of the scientists, Harry Daghlian, broke a safety rule. Despite an agreement not to work alone, he went to his laboratory that evening and proceeded to put together parts of a subcritical assembly. He was arranging some heavy uranium bricks that weighed about twelve pounds each. As he added the last brick, he accidently formed a low-grade critical assembly and received a lethal amount of radiation. Desperately, he separated the heavy bricks and in so doing his hands were burned. Daghlian died by inches over the the next twenty-four days. We learned of his suffering from those working in the hospital. It was a horrible death and sobering knowledge for those who learned about it. Our first death by radiation was an example of what was happening to thousands in Hiroshima and Nagasaki as a result of the work done at Los Alamos.

As many of us pondered over the tragedy of this death, the outside world continued praising the work of Los Alamos. Our mysterious "Shangri-La" had produced a community of heroes whose efforts had brought about the cessation of hostilities. It only remained for the terms of the surrender to be signed by the Japanese and Americans. Plans were already under way for the ceremony in Japan that would officially end the war.

A Manageable Crisis

Meanwhile, the reality that our "heroes" and their families were still living in a temporary, jerry-built environment, penetrated the excitement on our hill with the distribution of the following notice to every resident.

> "Attention all residents—Conserve water—We are now in the most crucial history of our water supply system. Recent rains have not helped at all and sources are decreasing at an alarming rate. Every person on the mesa must be water conscious and conserve water in every way possible to avoid the necessity of restrictions."

So, life on our hill went on its usual way. Where was the military that was going to see us through this crisis? Where were the Army Engineers who knew all the answers? What good were the reassurances from our general who had told us all summer that the military had the "situation well in hand?" Clearly, in regard to the community at Los Alamos, General Groves had one duty before all other—SAVE MONEY. He had counted on the population on our mesa remaining small and therefore requiring a limited demand for water. But the population had been growing steadily until Hiroshima Day. He hadn't seemed to notice the growing mob or to listen to the complaints of the swelling community. Perhaps, justifiably, he was busy with more important matters. Maybe if he didn't see or hear our petty problems, they would disappear.

At the time of the notice, there was water in our pipes. Though a little grey in color and reeking of chlorine, there *was* water. However, there was cause for apprehension. Our precious liquid sustenance came from a spring in Guaje canyon located in the Jemez mountains above and behind our hill. It was conveyed to our mesa in pipes laid carefully above the ground. Initially the pipes had been insulated, but some of the insulation had been chewed off long ago by unknown animals, maybe bears, wolves, or coyotes. I only know that some animals must have found the insulation simply delicious. We had been assured in the fall of 1944 that we could count on a heavy snow pack in winter to cover and insulate the pipes. But as the winter of 1944–45 gave way to spring, we learned that the snow pack in the mountains had been unusually light, certainly not heavy enough to cover the pipes. Moreover, there would be little runoff from that snow pack to fill the spring that supplied our water. As a result, there would be a light flow of water through the elevated, uninsulated pipes during the approaching winter. The water would very likely freeze in the pipes.

Water was stored in an old tower, a survivor from the original Los Alamos Ranch Academy. In winter, icicles hung from the tower. Children snapped them off and, "voila," had ice-cream cones! In summer, the tower offered welcome shade as we trekked to and from the commissary. It was the point from which we located our residences. It seemed to stand protectingly over us. And, now it was failing us.

Still, to some extent, the growing water shortage was a comforting reality. A water shortage, now there, I thought, was a problem we could handle—pretty well! It served as a focus for our irritability and tension. It was a welcome distraction from the bombardment of weightier news from the outside world. As summer of 1945 yielded to fall and then was replaced by winter, we handled the water shortage, in my recollection, with good humor and calm resignation. Here was a manageable, concrete problem. Our medical staff rose to the emergency and ordered everyone on the hill to have a series of inoculations to protect us from typhoid. Cheerfully, we lined up for our shots.

Our Own Little War

It was time to mend and to heal. The guns were quiet in the Pacific, and negotiators were hard at work planning what they hoped would be a lasting peace. We weren't doing so well right at home on the mesa. Our own little war between Fawn and the garbage men was heating up again. I watched the growing hostility with increasing concern. I was anything but a neutral observer, as I wrote to my parents:

Now Fawn has the spotlight again. Since he bit the garbage man, things have been getting worse. I've dutifully kept Fawn in the "clink" at trash collection times. Fawn is a real Jekyll-Hyde now. He's gentleness itself with the children, friends, and neighbors. Children can practically turn him inside out and climb all over him, and he stands for it. However, the garbage men have found it great sport to throw stones over our fence at a barking, raging Fawn. Now, Fawn just about goes insane when they arrive on the scene. He gnaws at the wire to get at them. I've asked them repeatedly to stop aggravating the dog and also to pass our house and not collect the garbage if Fawn happens to be out. They smilingly agree and continue throwing rocks. Yesterday when they were involved in their usual pastime, Fawn neatly vaulted over the fence and out. And garbage man number two was nipped. Fawn, the culprit, is now locked up at the vet's.

He was picked up by the vet's rather self-important assistant, a GI. I asked him what they did to second offenders. Dramatically, he bowed his head and said, "Ma'am, I hate to tell you. They have to do away with them." Lee got home about fifteen minutes after the GI left and found me in tears. He dashed over to the vet's and found out that the vet's assistant hadn't given us the facts quite straight. It did sometimes happen that animals were destroyed, but only at the owner's request. We were told that the health officer would call on me.

He did so the next day. It turns out that the health officer is none other than Dr. Barnett, Bobby's pediatrician, about the best-meaning, most sincere guy anyone would ever want to know. He was quite sympathetic. In fact, he told me that at this point there are three other dogs on the hill behaving exactly like Fawn. They will all get another chance. Dr. Barnett will get a big shot who speaks fluent Spanish to lecture the G-men on not stoning barking dogs, and on avoiding them when necessary. I have to watch Fawn carefully, but sooner or later, it will happen again. I'm so attached to that neurotic pup that I dread giving him up. They've done it, those darn garbage men, and I could just about chew them, too!

The Spanish-American who drives the bus for Leon's group [Leon worked at an area called "South Mesa," which was about six miles from the tech area; members of the group were transported from the tech area to and from "South Mesa" via Army bus] would like to take Fawn to live with him and his family on his ranch in the valley. I guess that's what we'll do.

Crossroads

We were beginning to look outside our hill for recreation
and needed purchases in addition to finding a home for Fawn.
Others were looking beyond our mesa, too. Most of the older
academic scientists, and "older" meant past thirty or so, had
positions to which they could return. Some had already
returned to their campuses as soon as the war ended. Some
of them were making plans to return to their posts for the fall
semester of 1946 at their respective universities. We began to
consider some basic alternatives, and I wrote about our preliminary dilemma.

> We're in the throes of thinking about our future. It's
> very clear that Lee either takes a university job and we
> starve or we eat heartily while Lee does research in indus-
> try. He has some interesting possibilities in regard to both
> and now the time has come to decide. Industrial jobs are
> being offered at almost twice what Lee earns now and some
> university jobs actually pay less! Anyway, we are at the
> crossroads now and so are our friends. All prefer university
> positions and all wonder how the dickens they can afford it.
> Conversations go like this: "Shall I enjoy starving at a
> university or shall I sell my soul to industry?"

Before that decision could be made and acted upon, one
thing was apparent. One year of desert and dust had taken
its toll on Leon's clothing. Like Fawn, Leon's baggy sport
coat would have to find another home in New Mexico.

Happily, the administration on the hill had sanctioned a
five-day work week (with no reduction in salary) as soon as
hostilities ceased. Weekend trips were now possible. We
wanted to take a short trip to Albuquerque and then, as soon
as Lee could get away, drive back to California for a visit
with our families. Aside from the question of clothes, a big
priority was for us to get off the mesa and celebrate. An

Albuquerque trip was, therefore, considered a necessity as well as a vacation. And, so I wrote:

> We may go to Albuquerque next weekend. We went over Lee's clothes, and he is almost ready for a barrel. We want to get him a sport coat, a good one this time, if possible.
>
> Santa Fe has only two stores. Both are awfully expensive and cater to Santa Fe summer tourists. So it's Albuquerque for us. Besides, we want to see Harold again and meet Chuck's wife, Betty, who is studying at the University of New Mexico in Albuquerque.

My next letter described the trip we took.

> Our Albuquerque trip was perfect. It offered a break from the excitement here and a chance to get our minds on other things besides the bomb, war and peace, and our future. We started Friday in the late afternoon. Jim (Keck), Chuck (Kunz) and Norman (Greenspan) went with us and, of course, Fawn. We carried clothing for everyone for the weekend, sandwiches and all sorts of supplies needed for our Bobby. We drove out the west gate and headed up the back road which is, reportedly, very picturesque. We soon discovered that the washboard, rock-strewn road was too bumpy for me. So we turned around and went back through Los Alamos. Then we drove along the well-worn, old traditional route to Santa Fe and on to Albuquerque. We must have been quite a sight. There were six of us plus a fox terrier in the muddiest car imaginable. We left Chuck at a small cottage where his wife was staying while studying at the university. Jim and Norman were deposited at a hotel. After scattering our load, we went to find Harold Shapiro, who was still at the university. Richard and Betty Bellman, already in Albuquerque, had been invited to meet us at Harold's.

Harold shares a very nice five-room house with another instructor, Marx Brook. Harold generously gave us his room, and he slept on the couch. Bobby was on the floor in the bedroom, and Fawn generally roamed. Richie, whom I described to you previously as the guy with the miserable, mistreated athlete's foot, was an absolute hero to Harold. Richie was an outstanding graduate student in mathematics at Princeton. Harold, also from Princeton (and a fine student as well), was simply overwhelmed to meet Richard (I think Harold was completely delighted to meet anyone he could really talk with after a year of isolation in New Mexico). You should have heard them reminisce at the top of their lungs! While we desperately looked around town for food, those two loudly recalled the "good old days." It was a little exasperating for starving me. Finally, we just gave up and straggled back, all of us, to Harold's place. Marx had company over, but we all managed to ignore them and they us. Harold got some sandwiches from a restaurant. I made spaghetti. Someone else got ice cream from somewhere. Betty Bellman went to her apartment and returned triumphant with wine and cranberry sauce, all she could find. The results were screwy, but filling, and the Bellmans, the Kunzes, the Fishers, Norman, Harold and Jim all ate heartily.

The next morning several of us went by car up into the Sandia range. This is a bony range of mountains east of Albuquerque. Harold sat in back of Leon, who was driving. Still exuberant, Harold kept turning to talk to Richie, who was also sitting in the back. The scenery, which was impressive, was totally lost on Harold. All the while he smoked a cigarette, gesturing as he talked. As we rounded a curve high in the mountains, Harold tried to throw his cigarette out through the driver's window. But the cigarette went down Leon's back instead. Lee let out a howl, jammed on the foot brake and jumped out of the still moving car. Jim managed to get the car to the side of the road, pulled the emergency brake, and was out of the car at once swatting Lee's back. Well, Lee didn't catch fire, the car didn't go over a cliff, and we all survived. But a stern and unsmiling Leon reorganized the seating and ordered, "No smoking." Jim, after peering anxiously over the edge of the road to a sheer drop below, lectured Harold and Richard on proper behavior while in a car, and we were off for the return trip down a winding dirt road back to Albuquerque. And that's how we celebrated the end of the war. We had survived the dangers of nuclear research and were almost done in by an innocent cigarette.

A picnic dinner by the Rio Grande completed our weekend. Somewhere between toasting the end of hostilities with red wine and munching on fried chicken, Lee realized that he had completely forgotten about looking for clothes. Oh, well, we decided, the baggy jacket would last a little longer.

Once back on the hill, we found that the mail had finally been sorted in the swamped tech area mail room. There was loads to read for everyone. Leon brought a pile home for us, as I wrote:

> It's really been amazing. We've actually been getting congratulatory letters from friends since the disclosure of the fact that we were making BOMBS.
>
> I just heard from Joan Livingston. Joan and her husband, Bob, are friends of ours from Berkeley days. They are at Oak Ridge, Tennessee. Joan and I have been corresponding since we left Berkeley. Right now it all seems completely ridiculous. Our letters have been so discreet and circumspect and foolish. The husbands have been doing related work, though I don't think Lee knew what Bob was doing at Oak Ridge or vice versa.

Reward for a Job Well Done

Early in the summer, Ben had left the mesa disguised as a civilian. At the time, Ben's departure had seemed very amusing to me. There was really nothing funny about it. In June of 1945, Ben had been selected from the SED group to go to Wendover Field, Nevada, to instruct Army Air Force officers who were to assemble the atomic bomb that was ultimately used over Nagasaki. Ben left the hill weeks before the Trinity test was held.

One minor problem had to be solved before he left Los Alamos. Ben, a lowly SED, would be training Army officers. He would be taking his meals at the officers' mess. In the hierarchical military set-up, no officer would ever take instruction from an NCO (non-commissioned officer). These plans had been made suddenly, and there hadn't been adequate time to think it all out. The only solution anyone could think of quickly was for Ben to go to Wendover disguised as a civilian. Ben, however, had no civilian clothes to wear, so he was given some money to purchase a basic wardrobe.

Later, on the day he was to leave, someone noticed that he was wearing regulation Army shoes, a dead give-away of his NCO status. Shoes were strictly rationed at that time, and he was instructed to rush to the security office for a permit that would lead to the acquisition of a shoe ration card necessary for purchasing shoes. He had little time to arrange this series of transactions as the afternoon bus was soon to leave for Santa Fe, where he had to buy the shoes before making connections for Wendover Field.

A WAC officer was ahead of him in the security office. Ben heard her complaining loudly and at length about her living quarters. It appeared that she had to share her dormitory accommodations with a group of young women from the Indian pueblos in the valley. She objected strongly.

Ben suddenly boiled over. For years, he figured, we had been fighting a war in Europe largely to erase the evils of virulent prejudice. He considered the WAC's statements to be bigoted and he told her so. The conversation quickly heated and apparently Ben used very strong language.

As he angrily expressed his opinions, he had quite an audience in the person of Major DeSilva, head of security. The major had his own temperamental outburst. But as he was a major and Ben a lowly SED, the result of the interchange was that Ben was "busted" on the spot to the rank of private, the lowest rank in the Army.

However, while in the process of being demoted, Ben got the permit, got the shoe ration, made the bus to Santa Fe, and bought a pair of shoes. Resplendent in his new clothes and burning from his demotion, Private Bederson was off in his civvies for Wendover Field. There he taught Army officers how to assemble parts of the atomic bomb destined for Nagasaki. During this period, as he lived in the officers' quarters and ate at the officers' club, he had to be careful to look and act like a civilian and above all remember not to salute officers.

Apparently all went well in Nevada, and Ben was sent with the officers to the island of Tinian, in the Pacific area, where the two bombs were assembled before being flown on their horrendous missions. Ben filled in the following details for me in 1984. Major DeSilva was also sent to Tinian as the officer in charge of security. The major was aware of Ben's work, both at Wendover and at Tinian, and realized what tension Ben must have been feeling on that hectic day as he had hurried in for a permit for a shoe ration card. It's a good guess that the major probably was also aware that he too had been feeling a good deal of anxiety at that time. He expressed regret at Ben's demotion and its inappropriateness and assured him that he would personally see to it that the recently demoted private would be promoted upward in rank as quickly as possible. Their work completed, the whole group at Tinian Island returned to a glorious welcome. That is, all but Ben, whose brief and glorious civilian experience was over. He headed back to barracks, mess hall, and the lowly position of a private in the Army until the promised promotion came through.

On October 16, 1945, Ben and the rest of the SEDs finally got some recognition but not the kind that they wanted. That was the day that an impressive and yet curious ceremony was held. In front of Fuller Lodge, one of the older buildings predating the project, a sort of reviewing stand had been erected. Red, white, and blue banners and bunting decorated the stand. Military officers were there in number, immaculate in their dress uniforms. A beaming, affable Robert Gordon Sproul, president of the University of California, was there resplendent in a double-breasted suit. To his left was General Groves, sober and dignified in a uniform that looked a little too tight. Sitting at the end of the row of dignitaries was Dr. Oppenheimer, looking strangely alone. In contrast to the others, Oppie was extremely thin and gaunt. Although he was over six feet in height, his weight had dropped to one hundred and fifteen pounds. He wore shabby clothes and his usual shapeless porkpie hat.

The purpose of the ceremony that day was the review and the rewarding of scientific achievement. We all gathered in front of the stand and sat on rows of folding chairs that had mysteriously appeared from somewhere. We had never *all* gathered anywhere before. There was a lot of animated conversation as we took our seats. We were very impressed with the mass view of ourselves. We were quite a crowd. We even looked neat, that is, down to our dust-covered shoes. I even heard an exultant "Real chairs with backs! We've arrived!" With the bunting-bedecked reviewing stand before us, the scene resembled Main Street, anywhere, on the Fourth of July. Bring on the marching bands!

No band appeared, but some soldiers marched in, quite smartly I thought, although I did see a general (I *think* he was a general) wince. Now we were ready for the ceremony. The big event was the presentation of the Army-Navy E (for

excellence) banner to the University of California, which
managed Los Alamos fiscally (and runs it to this day). Dr.
Sproul seemed oddly out of place, a crass outsider on our
hill, as he accepted the banner. He spoke briefly, and eloquently, as he always did, although I noted at the time that
people in the audience responded with perfunctory applause.
To all of us insular, parochial people, the thrill of the morning
was Oppie himself. He did not seem to be the least bit impressed with the award or anything that it signified. He took
the occasion to say what he felt so very, very deeply. As
I wrote:

> And what he said was so exactly what I've been feeling
> but have been unable to express. His talk was short, even
> faltering. He told us that the whole world must unite or
> perish. He felt that unless there is a way to prevent wars,
> the pride we are feeling today will give way to concern and
> fear for the future. He said that the day may come when
> "mankind will curse the names of Los Alamos and Hiro-
> shima."

To my surprise, I was similarly impressed by our general
when he addressed the assemblage.

> General Groves, too, was somber. He warned that there
> can be no effective defense against the A-bomb except to
> destroy the carrier before it arrives over a designated
> target. His hope is that we have a few years in which to
> get world cooperation and, if we succeed, then we are in a
> position to insure world peace.

He pointed out that we were at a crossroads in world
events. There was a clear choice between annihilation or
peace. We had only a short time. We'd better use that time
well. We listened attentively, proud of *our* general. Memories
of wood stoves, mud, and inadequate housing were mo-

mentarily forgotten. Today he was no longer our scapegoat or the butt of our jokes; he was *our* general. We hoped the other brass were suitably impressed.

Following these thought-provoking and sobering speeches, other awards were distributed. Lee was among those who received the Army-Navy E Award. We were pleased with the recognition the scientists received. However, Leon never did wear the pin that came with the award. But what about the SEDs? Would they get their due? The letter continues:

> Actually they *were* singled out. They were issued an insignia on a patch. The design was a horseshoe-shaped cluster of leaves. They were ordered to sew them on their uniforms. The disgusted SEDs immediately dubbed the badge "the order of the sanitary toilet seat" and many refused to affix them to their uniforms. Though some comments reached them about the excellence of their work, they remained convinced that they *really* were being cited for having the lowest venereal disease rate in the entire Army.

Ben and Normie were convinced of it. It figured, they reasoned. Their isolation was complete. Transportation was nonexistent. They simply had to have won "first prize." What an achievement!

The war, for the people on the hill, was officially over. The ceremony of closure on the horrendous product of the laboratories had been duly conducted. There followed a flurry of activity on the mesa. Many of the senior scientists left immediately for their tenured positions at their respective universities. Construction workers and machinists gathered up their families and left the hill in their weather-worn trailers. Oppenheimer returned to his faculty position at the University of California at Berkeley, and Norris Bradbury became acting director of the laboratory. Many of the younger staff started seriously searching for positions away from Los Alamos. A contented few elected to stay permanently and began to make plans to build homes in the hilly, wooded area surrounding our now muddy, now parched plateau.

Now that the war was over, some exciting changes took place in the tech area. An opportunity was given the staff to hear lectures by many of the luminaries on the hill. Courses were offered at the graduate level. Each scientist could sign up for two courses during the working day. Leon was thrilled and felt it was the opportunity of a lifetime and attended superb lectures given by Edward Teller and Hans Bethe.

It was a nice way to mark time while the future of the laboratory was uncertain. And rumors flourished as to the future of the site. Some (Oppenheimer included) felt strongly that Los Alamos had outlived its usefulness and should be completely closed down. We should all flee as quickly as possible, as had the Indians of long ago in the neighboring Frijoles Canyon. The area should be suitably fenced in. The jeeps should be left to sink gracefully into the mud, the barracks and miserable housing left to decay. Appropriately trained guides could escort tourists around the ruins.

There were others who felt just as strongly that the facility should be converted into a peaceful research center. The peaceful utilization of nuclear power should be developed, and the laboratories should be opened to all types of research. Still others argued that nuclear research should be continued, preferably on an international basis, perhaps under the auspices of the United Nations. Still others reasoned that a strong American arsenal of nuclear weapons might be the best, or only, insurance of peaceful survival on this planet.

As we argued on our hill, I began to feel that my own name for the site, Shangri-La, was most inappropriate. For me, the name of Shangri-La at first had fit our initially remote, cocoon-like existence which was no more. In the fall of 1945, Los Alamos was no imaginary retreat from the realities of life in our troubled world. Rather, we represented, in a microcosm, the viewpoints of many parts of our civilization. Maybe we were more like the patients in the tuberculosis sanitarium described by Thomas Mann in *The Magic Mountain*. These hospitalized patients on their "magic mountain" debated and theorized in their splendid isolation, while surrounded by beautiful scenery. As they argued, the countries below their mountain were preparing for World War I, which suddenly exploded all around their sanctuary. Were we doing the same thing?

8. *Harvest Time*

Neighborhood Doings

ONE SUNNY MORNING I INSPECTED our car thoroughly. That means I kicked the four tires. As none popped open or exploded, I figured that our grimy car was good for at least one more trip to Santa Fe. So, off we went, three pregnant women with our three small sons.

Minnie, Rhuby Jean, and I took our three boys and the Fisher car to Santa Fe today. We prayed all the way, as our tires are pretty sad and it will be a while before we can get new ones. On the way down our gravelly road from the mesa, we made a decision. If we had a flat tire en route, we would merely get out of the car and line up along the road. No one could help but be moved to compassion at the sight of three very pregnant females and a limping car! Rhuby Jean expects her baby in three weeks, Minnie in December, and I am practically sure little "Hoo" won't arrive until January. And each of us with a little laddie of from one and a half to three! The waitress at the De Vargas, where we had lunch, asked calmly, "Well, you all have boys now; do you all want girls this time?"

We made it down and back without mishap. [Certainly our judgment in making the trip might be questioned.] It had been marvelous to go to Santa Fe and not feel the wall of silence between us and the town people. It was fun to be friendly for a change with the Santa Feans who were eager to talk to us. At any rate, we returned happy and starved.

Once back on the hill there was no time to go to the commissary or to make dinner.

On our return, Minnie, Bill, their Billy and we Fishers had dinner together at the cafeteria. Right near us sat Dr. Stout, our obstetrician, his wife and child. We had served ourselves gargantuan meals. Minnie felt she had gained too much weight already. She was afraid to eat! Minnie said she was tempted to remark loudly, "No, no potatoes for me, please." We sort of hid our chocolate sundaes.

So far I've gained about eight pounds, which is surprisingly low, considering all the eating I've been doing. Minnie has gained thirty-five pounds, and I *am* impressed. She gained that much before and lost it after Billy was born. She doesn't worry about it at all, although Dr. S. just about tears his hair out whenever she comes in for an appointment.

I think all our talking over the months about cars and their troubles has finally gotten to Bobby. Lately he has gone limping around the house. When questioned as to why, he remarks, "I'm a flat tire," and limps on. He also puts water "in my road-er-ater" [radiator] when he drinks. Then I hear him limp off saying a mixture of, "Down a hill, five gallons for me, chug, chug, we're stuck, backing up now." He gets the picture!

Pressure was decreasing in the labs and Leon was relaxing. Someone in his lab who was leaving the project passed on his swivel chair to Leon. Well, to Lee it was a wonderful toy. Round and round he went until he felt dizzy. Then he stopped, relaxed, leaned back and fell over backwards. Clearly, it went to his head in more ways than one! As a result:

Lee came home today with a stiff neck and shoulder. He explained to me what had happened and it all seemed so amusing. I couldn't help laughing, which was very offensive

to one practically on his deathbed. He had a heat treatment
this afternoon, and a lovely WAC gave him a massage,
which made him much happier. Now does his military.
hospital medical record state "injured by a swivel chair"?
Anyway, I hope he recovers by the time we move.

It was at this time that Leon received an increase in pay
for "doing hazardous work." It was Jim who remarked upon
hearing about the raise, "The only way you could hurt
yourself is by poking yourself in the eye with a pencil."
"Or," I added, "by falling over backwards in a swivel chair!"

We may move next week or the week after that (as
Hoo's expected arrival qualifies us for a larger house). I
have picked out a house—if! It is a McKee house like ours
and has no fireplace, but we'll manage somehow. The
large units with fireplaces have four apartments each. The
heat is centrally controlled and a worse problem than our
miserable system. We'll have an extra room and two more
closets. What's the "if"? The house is next to a large
ditch. I've said I'll only take it if they fill in the ditch.
They (the mysterious military) said they would see what
could be done. That is where it stands now. I'm waiting
for men with shovels to materialize, or maybe even a
bulldozer. We'll let you know next week.

Looks as though I'm giving a Thanksgiving dinner again
this year. The fellows are asking about another. I hope
we're moved by then and have the electric oven. Otherwise
I will have to roast the turkey half at a time in my miniature kerosene contraption and with highly unpredictable
results.

For once something went as planned. A group of men
(five) with shovels (three) took turns filling in the ditch.
We moved around the end of October to a house about 200
feet from the house we had just left. No longer did we have

the view of the mountains across the desert, but we were only a short distance from our group of friends. We were settled quickly and were soon comfortable and happy in our new (for us) home. These relatively spacious accommodations had been recently vacated by Frank Oppenheimer, brother of the director. Lee happily took over one room as a study, which he planned to relinquish to little "Hoo" upon his arrival. But it wasn't all friendship and cheer on our new street. As I wrote:

> Our new neighborhood does have its problems. In general, my new neighbors are terrific, but there is one awful exception. The people diagonally across the road couldn't be much worse. They scream at each other and actually beat their kids. A couple of days ago their three-year-old boy wandered, though forbidden to, out into the street, and his mother threw him against the house and left him screaming in the dirt. I was so furious I could have thrown her, except that she is quite tall and I'm kind of off balance. Then, I noticed Bobby watching the performance with tears in his eyes. He said over and over, "Poor Warren, poor Warren."
>
> Today, I called Bobby into the kitchen to taste something I had just made. When he heard me call him, he shouted, "What's eating you?"—which we hear across the street. Now he has picked up a really bad word that we're busy discouraging. I know where he heard it. The other neighbors are pretty upset about this family. No one knows what to do.

There was no children's protective society to report to or from which to get help. In our isolated community, there were no resources for a warring couple or for parents who had family problems. Even if those people had wished to seek help, there was none. So, not knowing what to do, we gossiped, sighed, and did nothing.

Early November brought snow. The water shortage was

being handled in typical Army style with continuing notices to residents and workers to conserve water. We were advised to save the water from bathing the baby and use it to wash our floors, shower only when necessary, and flush toilets as seldom as possible.

Electric outages were common, too, as more and more power was utilized on the hill. It was hard for us who were not employed on the hill to understand why, with the bombs completed and the work of the hill essentially done, more and more power seemed to be needed. The Army developed a solution for the outages with the same skill with which it had handled the water shortage. It divided the residential areas into two parts. Alternately, current was fed to one or the other area. In our homes, lights were replaced by candles, which were then replaced by lights every half-hour as the power went on and off. On several occasions, during a candlelit period, Leon would go outside and read the paper illuminated by our automobile headlights. Those who were fortunate enough to have electric plates for cooking had to plan carefully in order to use their appliances on the hour or on the half-hour, depending upon their location on the mesa. Dinners were delayed; nerves were frayed. The much maligned "black beauties" suddenly developed a patina and a charm and the blackened, smoky kerosene stoves were newly appreciated as they defied the electrical shortage and reliably belched forth cooked meals.

At the laundries, washing machines, choked with suds and clothing, took regular half-hour siestas, giving the irritated wives thirty full minutes of time to lambast our general. The temperature in our flimsy houses took recurrent half-hour dips when the fans that circulated the heat from our furnaces were suddenly and repeatedly immobilized. We were assured that the power would stay on at night in order to run those fans. It took more than electric power, however, as one of my letters home indicated:

This morning we woke up freezing. Our heat was off and had been off for hours. Lee went out to investigate the problem and discovered that we were completely out of oil. (Keeping the tank outside filled with heating oil is the project's responsibility, not ours.) While I dressed Bobby in his snow suit, Lee went to the housing office for help. He tried. Nothing happened! We went through the morning without heat. Lee came home for lunch expecting to find us snug and warm. We weren't! He was really disgusted. He went back to the housing office and found that the wrong desk had gotten his message. No one in the office had noticed the note or had bothered to relay the message to the next desk where it belonged. Late this afternoon, we finally got our oil. The smiling Spanish truck driver explained the situation to us, saying, "I had the inflooza [influenza] vera-bad. Seek a bed. My men, they no work. Hokay now."

Well, "Hokay" for now! I was beginning to wish that I had selected one of the four apartment complexes that had a fireplace. But I had really been discouraged from such selection by Bernice [Brode] who lives in one of the greenhouse complexes. She gave me the feeling that those residents live in constant fear of fire. Sometimes the temperature in their tinder boxes has reached ninety degrees. She reports that the furnace men stoke and stoke coal like mad. The apartments turn into roasting ovens. Better to freeze now and then, I decided.

Thanksgiving Warmth

November days were crisp and cold but beautiful. The Sangre de Cristo range across the valley was once again snow-covered and glowed almost red in the sunset. Mud-caked cars were descending our hill for their last time and heading towards those glowing mountains as the exodus from the mesa continued. The days were filled with poignant farewells and promises to keep in touch. The closeness and camaraderie we had experienced during months of isolation was dissipating. We were left with a sense of emptiness and loss.

My reaction at that time was to cling to outside contacts. I wrote for information, for supplies, and ordered the *New York Times* to be mailed to us. I wrote repeatedly for news from the outside world, and reestablished contact with college friends now scattered all over the country. I tried repeatedly to encourage my sister Shirley and her husband Bob to come to Santa Fe where we could visit them, but to no avail.

The New York Times was a mixed blessing. Part of the news of the outside world involved some unanswered questions about conditions in Hiroshima and Nagasaki. Was the land still radioactive? Would trees grow again? How many people were dying from radiation sickness? Would the newborn United Nations have the strength to prevent future wars? All this was anxiety-provoking reading.

I had always been able to escape anxieties through music. Escape was a necessity at Los Alamos. I found refuge from worries when singing with the struggling choral society. At this time our little local chorus, more famous for its enthusiasm than its musical talent, was rehearsing Handel's oratorio, "The Messiah." We met regularly in the evenings, a small group of perhaps thirty. A few of the better singers were asked to take solo parts, and a narrator filled in where the music was too difficult for an untrained soloist. I was the only pregnant chorister. I was enthusiastic about the chorus and its efforts (though not necessarily the results). I particularly loved singing "For unto Us a Child is Born" as I felt the tiny life stirring within me. And choral members shared my delight and some of my dilemmas. As I wrote:

I just returned from a "Messiah" rehearsal, and I still feel silly about the whole thing. Tonight we had some very important decisions to make as to what we'll wear for the concert. First, the director asked who wouldn't be there for the performance. (Rumors are spreading that some military personnel will be asked to leave the hill for a while if the water shortage becomes more acute.) Hilda [Condit] cheerfully volunteered, after looking me over, that I may not make it to the performance. Which was nice of her! Then formals were decided upon, and it was agreed that we just saunter in. I decided to be in the audience at that point. Then, fellow sopranos reconsidered and rallied with happy ideas such as finding a barrel in a long model, or adding some black material to the bottom of my dress. It got sillier and sillier. Someone offered me some blackout material (what was blackout material doing at Los Alamos, so far from our shores?), which I haven't accepted as yet. I suggested we try to get choir robes from Santa Fe. That is under consideration. Hilda then suggested we make a formal of sorts for me out of her cap and gown, which for some crazy reason is here on the hill in a box in her apartment. And that is when we deferred the discussion until next week. Stand by, and learn how this difficult problem is solved!

Well, a few other similarly "difficult" problems needed solving around that time. A Thanksgiving turkey had to be procured and prepared. Back in civilization, that's no problem. On an Army post such as ours, however, nothing happened as planned. As I wrote:

We've had a hilarious day over the acquisition of our turkey. I went happily to the commissary only to discover to my dismay that the project had procured a supply of turkeys each weighing 25 to 28 pounds. There were none smaller. The Army Quartermaster was blissfully under the impression that the turkeys were all for delivery to mess halls. We civilians had been completely forgotten. Besides, the turkeys were very frozen and it was impossible to cut them in half. Finally, after scouting around, I found a woman willing to split one (how?) with me. Somehow, between us, we got the monster home to my house, lugged it through the living room and deposited it on the kitchen counter where, hopefully, it would thaw out.

Lee arrived home for lunch and almost collapsed in horror at the sight of the mammoth bird. He explained that that he had just asked a GI who was going to Santa Fe to do a favor for him while in town, and buy a 14-pound turkey for our dinner. Furthermore, Lee had phoned the butcher shop and had one reserved for us. After a hurried consultation with me, he dashed out of the house with the huge carcass and found the woman I planned to share it with. She decided to substitute chicken for her Thanksgiving. On to the commissary! Here he managed to get permission to return the turkey.

Fine planning so far. Except—it's evening now and up to this time the GI who had gone to Santa Fe has not returned with our 14-pound turkey. Tomorrow, being Thanksgiving Day, the commissary will be closed. Maybe we'll have scrambled eggs for dinner!

Soon after I finished the above letter, the awaited GI sauntered in, tired and a little drunk. He had the turkey with him and our evening was saved! Our guests were SEDs, Richard, Normie, Chuck, Murray and Jim. For once I wasn't the only woman at the table. Richard's wife Betty managed to come up on the hill for the first time and join us. The party also included Peggy Ramsay, a friend of Jim's that I had not met. I liked her at once. Peggy, a delightful down-to-earth redhead, was a physicist who worked on the hill. During the day, practically all the above-mentioned guests dropped in at some time or other to smell dinner cooking.

Winter's Chill

The following evening, films were shown of Hiroshima and Nagasaki. At that meeting, scientists who had gone to those cities after the war to investigate the bombs' effects reported in a matter-of-fact way about the swath of destruction, the burn statistics, and then turned to radiation injuries and deaths. They told of the lingering effects of radiation and described the symptoms of the bombs' long-term effects. We learned that people were dying by inches, dying of radiation sickness. They would be dying for years to come. Oppie, looking wasted and sickly on his brief return to the hill, reminded the group that there was no acceptable alternative to seeking a moral solution to the control of atomic bombs and that time already was running out. All the happiness of Thanksgiving, all the warmth and glow of a lovely evening, drained from me as I listened to facts, to figures, and then to Oppie. I was appalled. The world had gone mad.

From that evening on, it was hard to erase the pictures of Hiroshima and of Nagasaki from my mind. Now I had seen films showing miles of charred devastation. I had seen adults with screams frozen on their faces, children lost in the rubble, babies with stunned expressions on their faces.

Besides, I was feeling poorly. My head kept aching. My stomach was continuously upset. Naturally I took my complaints to the doctor. Leon wrote the next letter to my parents and tried to sound as reassuring as possible.

Phyllis hasn't written you for so long that I thought I would drop you a line. Phyllis isn't feeling just right. Several days ago, she complained of a severe thumping at one spot on her head. She began to have dizzy feelings and pretty bad nausea. The upshot of it all is that the doctor asked her to spend a little time in the hospital. He feels very sure that the whole thing can be cleared up in a day or so with proper attention. She went to the hospital today, and they allowed nothing in her stomach, not even water, but fed her intravenously. The doctor feels that if she can keep food down tomorrow, everything will be OK. He thinks it is toxemia, which usually comes with edema, which she also had when pregnant with Bobby. The doctor says that it was caught so early there is nothing at all to worry about. She might be home tomorrow night.

In the meantime, Bobby stays at nursery school from 8:00 A.M. till 3:30 P.M. and has his lunch there. Neighbors take him until 6:30 when I get home. A girl comes in the evening, bathes Bobby and helps out until 9:30. I go off to visit Phyllis around 7:30.

I feel sure she is OK. She has a lot of confidence in her doctor, and he has been in to see her many, many times already. She is in the maternity ward. Everybody congratulates her on having had the baby!

Please don't let this letter alarm you. I just feel you would like to know what is going on. I will write you tomorrow with further news.

The next day, Lee informed my parents that I was still in the hospital and feeling pretty discouraged. He managed to bring Bobby to the hospital window to visit me. I remember that visit very clearly. The following day I managed a letter home myself, a letter that was full of complaints.

Dr. Stout hasn't been in yet this morning. I'm pretty sure he'll let me go home today. I feel *much* better and can eat like a regular person again. It wasn't much fun. I had such headaches and was so dizzy. Any food that went down came back up. My back was aching. My hands and feet were swollen.

The hospital is fine; the nurses are wonderful. But, I sort of resent the cooing mothers around me and also the fact that I'll leave the hospital looking exactly as I did when I came in.

All the packages you sent arrived a couple of days ago. Thanks. But, where are the baby clothes? Dad, you said you would get two dozen diapers from your store. I'll need them soon.

Bobby has started nursery school. He was unceremoniously *dumped* there when I landed in the hospital.

I meant this literally. Lee was in such a hurry to get to work that he actually handed Bobby to someone over the nursery school fence and dashed off. My sudden hospitalization meant that there was no opportunity to introduce Bobby to the school gradually as had been planned. The school staff was accustomed to the sudden arrival of new children, for the school was routinely the repository for preschoolers whenever there was any sort of emergency.

There had been another change in Bobby's short life just two weeks before. Fawn, the "terror of the mesa" to the garbage men, had gone to live down in the Pojoaque valley with Manuelo, a Los Alamos bus driver. This left our house strangely quiet and peaceful at garbage collection time, but left a heartbroken little Bobby behind. My complaining letter continues:

And, this is what I resent! When we gave Fawn away a couple of weeks ago, Bobby soaked his bed for a week. When I came here, he only soaked his bed two nights! When Lee brought him to the window last night, Bobby made it clear he resented my being here. Lee had said to him, "We'll go see Mommy and then we'll go and see the ducks." When Bobby saw me he said a brief "Hi," and then turned to his Daddy and said, "And now let's go see the ducks." I tried to explain that I *had* to stay here until I was well enough to go home but he wouldn't even look at me.

We have just heard that all censorship has been lifted. It looks as though we soon can have visitors for the day, week, or whatever. I'm sort of restricted as to activity and diet, but we could have a great visit anyway. Please think seriously about coming. We'll try to phone you Sunday.

Why was I so depressed at this time? It was a time when I should have been very happy. The war was over. Leon wouldn't be drafted. My baby was due in a month. In retrospect, it seemed that my anxiety had started before "Trinity," probably at the time when we were trying to think of names for our little "Hoo." This anxiety changed to depression about the time I viewed the films of Hiroshima and Nagasaki. It took the form of a sense of futility and helplessness. There was no way to defuse those feelings, which only accelerated as my friends and I burdened each other with our worries. I needed outsiders and I needed them badly. My letters home reflected my feelings of inadequacy and need. My usual attempt to hide problems with humor was wearing thin. Too often the attempt at humor was tinged with sarcasm.

Minnie had her baby the day I left the hospital. A mere nine-pound boy, that's all. Up here, it seems as though if you have one under seven pounds they throw 'em back! Minnie is fine and ate a huge meal right afterwards. She didn't have a hard time at all. I kept her company through her labor until I left [the hospital]. She was giddy and gay the whole time. I drooled with envy.

Other news is that the ration board has come to life. We were told we can get permission to purchase retreaded tires next week. We talked to Mr. Miller, manager of the garage in Santa Fe. He will go to Albuquerque with our order and get us tires as quickly as he can find them. He goes down weekly for supplies. "Meanwhile, up at the ranch," when Lee came to get me at the hospital, another tire went blooey. Now we can't drive our car at all.

We think it would be tons of fun if you could come up and visit us, possibly over New Year's. How about it?

Rules have finally been relaxed. Censorship is no more and we can have visitors *provided* that they are cleared by Army intelligence. So, if you think there is even a possibility of your coming, tell us so we can start them investigating to their dear little hearts' content. You'll have to bring plenty of identification, social security cards, driver's licenses, all you can collect. We have to know just when to expect you. A pass will be waiting for you at the outer gate. It would be a quiet vacation for all of us, necessarily so, but there is still plenty that you could do. Anyway, when people first come up to this altitude, they are always cautioned to take it easy. Visitors are limited as to where they can go up here; but there is plenty of leeway. You wouldn't feel like captives. You'd see some lovely country, snow, us, Bobby and maybe (why maybe?) if you stick around, a new arrival.

Lee is taking over his authority and has given me orders to get to bed. Oh, the buggy is beautiful and so is the bathinette. We're grateful to you for sending them here. Only trouble is, and it isn't a very major one, that the wind- or storm-shield for the buggy is supposed to have four hooks to hold it in place. They weren't included. We looked carefully. Lee could probably get some hooks made here somehow, but he'd rather not if it isn't necessary. But, the clothing is *still* to arrive. WHEN? Lee says, "Get to bed," and here I go.

Nothing seemed to go as planned. For one thing, Bobby's nursery school didn't meet my standards. Rosemary, the director of the school, had just left the hill. The building housing this program was small and flimsy. The equipment was minimal and the teaching staff randomly selected. This selection was based upon the assumption that if you had produced children you were automatically skilled enough to be a nursery school teacher.

The overworked, underpaid and untrained teachers did

their very best, but the general effect in the crowded nursery schoolrooms was one of free-flowing confusion. The teachers tried valiantly to bring order out of chaos. Certainly Sally Flanders did. One morning I visited the school and when I learned that two of the staff hadn't appeared due to illness, I stayed to help. I found Sally seated at the piano and in the small room about fifteen tots were marching around in a circle.

As Sally played enthusiastically, one little tyke, a girl of about three-and-a-half, called out, "It's too loud!"

Sally whirled around on her stool and asked, "Well, can you do better?"

"No," mumbled the child.

"OK, then you march; I'll play," said Sally.

Sally explained later that the morning had gotten off to an impossible start. Two new children had started school that day and started as precipitously as had our Bobby. One little youngster was still in a state of utter misery and required the complete attention of one of the teachers. Two kiddies had temperature elevations requiring someone to come and get them. A tarantula had been found in the nursery school play area. I got the point. I was needed to track down the parents of the sick children. So, off I went.

Without telephones in the homes, communication with parents or absent teachers was severely handicapped. Telephone messages went to the tech area to husbands who brought the information home to their wives. The reply to the message went the reverse route. Carrier pigeons might have worked better.

Little Bobby, whose development and activities had always been a source of joy to his doting mother, wasn't needing me so much. In fact I couldn't even tell him stories, or so it seemed.

Times have changed. We no longer can tell Bobby a story. We get the first sentence out, and then he tells the rest. It's really funny. All of a sudden, he's gotten interested in nursery rhymes and can say five in a row, all at once, hardly stopping for breath. Then he "reads" his own books solemnly word for word, and "No help" needed.

My letter went on to describe another problem.

I'm enclosing an announcement of a very sad state of affairs. The water shortage has grown more serious. I hope it will be alleviated by the time you both come up. We still expect you. It is all pretty much arranged with the exception that all visitor passes may be cancelled due to the water situation.

Now as to the water. Dirty water drips through our taps. We have filled our washing machine with the grimy stuff and use it to flush the toilet. We go to a distribution center to get clean water from trucks coming up from the valley. This isn't so bad on us, but pity those with infants. My only hope is that by the time Hoo arrives we'll have water again.

On December 19, a special announcement concerning the water shortage was distributed to all residents. I found the message grim and at the same time humorous. As censorship had been recently removed, I sent a copy of the notice to my parents. Included in the terse message from Colonel Seeman, commanding officer of the post, were my scribbled comments (in parentheses).

SPECIAL ANNOUNCEMENT
IMPORTANT
The water situation may continue indefinitely due to weather conditions beyond our control. (Ever hear of weather conditions *within* our control?) If and when the water may be on temporarily it is recommended you fill such containers as you may have at home.

Water *is* being hauled by truck, but these quantities are
far below normal requirements.

Most of the industrial use is being stopped, but it is
mandatory that steam plants keep operating to avoid further freezing. (Lee's lab is heated, or was heated, by steam
and he now freezes at work.)

Fire protection and sanitation are of first importance.
Be especially watchful for fires. (What do we do if we see
one? Without water? Watch?) Stoppage of toilets must be
avoided, so give this your close attention, also the hospital
has first priority on hauled water. (What a sentence!)

We must suspend all bathing except emergency. (When
does it become an emergency? Bill Ogle suggests "stinko-
meters" to be placed, one in the tech area and one at the
commissary. They should be so constructed that when your
stink passes a certain point and when you pass a certain
point, a bell will ring. The happy winner will get a card
entitling him to one shower! Oh, there are endless possibilities. Take a nice warm lingering bath before you come!
Maybe Apolonia has water in her pueblo. On the other
hand, maybe not!)

Trucks will haul both potable and untreated water. Use
the first for drinking and cooking. Use the latter in pails
for flushing toilets. Do not waste any. Provide yourselves
with carrying containers for both types of water. Do not
mix them.

Trucks for both types of water are parked between the
Hospital and Water Tower. (Pretty embarrassing for the
water tower.) Containers may be filled there. As more
trucks are procured parks will be established at other
central points. (Oh well, at least they still collect garbage
and we do have electricity—now and then. One shouldn't
complain!)

Despite my pleas, and to my disappointment, my father
didn't plan to travel to Los Alamos. He wrote that he could

not be away from his business at that time of year. He owned
and managed two women's apparel stores. Christmastime was
his busiest time. Around New Year's Day, he ran a huge
sale. Then inventory must be taken, taxes and other matters
worked out, and the books closed for the year. (As I write
this I can't help but wonder if the water shortage scared
him off.)

But, my mother would be happy to come. She was eager to
visit us, calm her worries about my health, greet Hoo, and see
the fabled Los Alamos first hand. I was feeling a little more
cheerful as she made plans to arrive soon after the first of the
year.

Festivities

Christmas was almost upon us. We joined with others on the
hill in making preparations for the holiday. Why was a Jewish
family at Los Alamos celebrating Christmas? In those days,
many Jewish families in San Francisco, although they retained
their Jewish identity, celebrated Christmas as a secular holiday
as did their neighbors around them. Maybe it was an attempt
to "fit in" with the customs of a predominantly Christian
society. Maybe it was incongruous, as "fitting in" hadn't
saved Jewish society in Germany, where the Jews had been
highly assimilated into German culture before the advent of
Hitler. At Los Alamos, in particular, there was no Jewish
alternative. There was no synagogue, and to my recollection,
no evidence of Jewish worship, and no organized way to join
together to celebrate Jewish holidays.

At any rate, to start the season off, Handel's "The
Messiah" was performed by our little chorus on December
21, on our wedding anniversary. So we celebrated by Phyllis
singing and Leon listening in the audience. The concert was
performed in Theatre II, our multi-purpose building. The
audience was enthusiastic, if uncritical, and I needn't have

worried about being conspicuously pregnant, as my letter relates:

Friday night, the fourth anniversary of our marriage, was also the night of the "Messiah" performance. First, I'll explain that due to the water situation it was announced the day before the concert that SEDs could take immediate emergency furloughs for two weeks. So the day before the event we found ourselves lacking a clarinet, a bassoon, two cellos, and a violin, as well as being reduced to only three tenors! We held an emergency meeting to decide how to handle this new crisis and decided to give the concert anyway. We were all asked to sing tenor parts whenever we weren't struggling to handle our own parts. Actually, it wasn't too bad and I needn't have worried about feeling conspicuous. I was safely hidden in the second row and sang along happily. Lee says he couldn't see me at all, not even my face. I stood next to Hilda Condit who is about five feet eight inches. Next to her was Sally Flanders who, I'm positive, must be almost six feet tall. Jim, Murray, and Norman also saw only a space where I should have been. Compared with Hilda and Sally I didn't even exist!

At the intermission, Bob Dike, the conductor, signaled the soloists to rise and bow. We had expected this. However, one of the three "surviving" tenors decided to play a trick on me. He told me that Bob had changed his mind and at the signal we *all* were to rise. Bob signaled, and up I went with the soloists—almost, as Hilda grabbed me just in time!

As a contribution towards the festive season, a group of GIs, freed from their now unnecessary guard duty, had been sent out to the woods to cut trees. Our woods were wooded, you might say, but with singularly scrawny pines. The GIs did their best and found a few shapely "Christmas" trees, which were set up at Fuller Lodge and several other communal buildings. The others, a thin, gaunt collection, were distributed to residents around the mesa. The trees were decorated with whatever was at hand. There was no tinsel. It had gone the way of other war-appropriated commodities. There were no lights. The electrical shortage prohibited their usage. So we improvised with what was on hand.

Our tree looks fine to me, but Bobby isn't quite satisfied. I made great strings of alternating cranberries and pop-corn and tied on brightly painted pine cones. I thought the effect was splendid. We showed the results proudly to Bobby the next morning and he surveyed it critically. We asked him how he liked it and he replied, "Pretty good." Then he added sadly, "No lights." He had seen the real thing in Santa Fe, a nice, fat, beautifully decorated tree complete with lights, ornaments, and tinsel. I think that was what he expected. Sorry about that, little boy! Our skinny, limp, crooked tree will just have to do.

Our holiday fun was dimmed by a bad accident. Joyce, age eight, was in her home alone. The little girl decided to melt some paraffin and did a fine job of setting the works on fire. Mary saw the smoke, dashed into Joyce's house, got the pot and was pretty badly burned getting the stuff out of the house. I took Mary right to the hospital where the doctors had to give her morphine. We contacted Dot and Scotty, the girl's parents, and they came right home and spanked poor Joyce. I was so darn mad! She is only eight and shouldn't be left home alone. As they both work, she is home alone after school every day. They should be so thankful that their little girl is alive and unhurt!

9. *Learning New Lessons*

A New School Principal

A S I HAVE EXPLAINED, the Los Alamos nursery school was swamped with little toddlers crowded into an inadequate building. The public school, on the other hand, stood firm and imposing, was well equipped and practically empty. The building itself was of superior construction. It was, in fact, much finer than it needed to be, certainly far superior in construction to anything else on our hill. Its costs skyrocketed during construction, much to the chagrin of our penny-pinching general. It had been built in 1943 according to specifications routinely required for a *permanent* Army base school. One requirement was that it be built on a solid cement foundation. Not a bad idea, but the construction crew discovered that the site selected for the school was solid rock. They blasted the rock and installed a cement foundation, blindly following the instruction manual to the letter. It should have been obvious that the solid rock would have made a fine foundation. No need for the cement!

The school building was "first-class" all the way through, inappropriately, incongruously so. It was anticipated that the students would all be first-class as well. An educator hired by the Manhattan District had made a preliminary survey and predicted the need for a school for superior children. Following the survey an elite school had been planned for the children of a highly educated staff.

Apparently he hadn't taken a hard look at the realities of planning a school for a community such as ours. He couldn't have really studied the potential makeup of the school. As a result, the school was unprepared to meet the needs of the actual student population. In 1943 the upper school contained, all told, forty students. Of these, eight were children of the technical staff, a few more were children of the construction crew. The majority were the children of the Spanish-American workers. These families had lived in the valley below, before moving up to our hill. They had no tradition of education and saw little value in it. They wanted their children to learn a trade. In most cases the parents spoke only Spanish. Their children were bilingual, having learned English in the schools in the valley. The staff members' children were not out-standing scholars, but nevertheless had plans of continuing on to college. They needed a curriculum that would prepare them for college admission. Few of the other children planned or hoped to pursue their education beyond high school.

There was no summer program for the children up on the mesa and, consequently, the teenagers ran wild all summer. In the fall, teachers were overwhelmed with the task of corralling these young ones and transforming them into stu-dents. In addition, the teachers were ill-equipped for their roles. The military had decreed that teachers be selected from the many excellently educated wives on the hill, and forbade importing teachers from outside of Los Alamos. It was true that there were excellently educated women on the hill. Some who taught at school had Ph.D. degrees, but they generally lacked prior classroom experience. No one on the staff knew how to *run* a school. And the kids knew it! The supposedly "elite" school became, instead, a major disaster area. Discipline was a constant problem. Student absenteeism was excessive. One teacher, Alice Smith, complained one day that her class had been sadly depleted "down to seven." Somehow a group of teenagers had left the school, appropriated an Army truck, and gone off to Santa Fe!

The teachers worked desperately. Jane Wilson taught English. In college, she had been an English major. The chemistry teacher died of polio while on the hill and she was never replaced. There was no physics teacher until after the war was over. Occasionally a technician gave a talk or a demonstration. That had to suffice until after August 6, 1945, when scientists from the tech area, one by one, donated time to the school and set up a physics course.

Foreign languages were introduced as extra-curricular activities. Two wives willing to teach French and Latin, Peg Bainbridge and Francoise Ulam, both had tiny babies. They had to find time to teach between infant feedings. But every day, Spanish was being spoken all around us. Yet no instruction in Spanish was available for students. Among all the Spanish-Americans on our hill we might have found several with teaching skills. Failing that, an English-speaking teacher and a Spanish-speaking resident could have worked as a team. If we couldn't teach the languages traditionally taught in American public schools (French, German, Latin), we had a rare and wonderful opportunity to teach our children conversational Spanish.

Some of the residents on the hill who had come from Berkeley had known Margery Crouch there, and knew her reputation as a teacher and disciplinarian. Whether or not anyone knew anything about her philosophy of education, let alone agreed with it, was immaterial. She was clearly the only one to bring order out of scholastic chaos. An exception was made to the "hiring on-hill teachers only" rule and Margery was sent for. She was met at Lamy by Bernice Brode in an official Army car. As they wound their way up to the mesa, Marge learned for the first time that she had been hired not as a teacher but to be principal of the high school. She was appalled. She had only taught lower grades and had absolutely no administrative experience. As Marge looked apprehensively at the cliffs and chasms ahead, Bernice told her about the problem-beset Los Alamos school. Marge arrived on the hill to find the school board in session and waiting for her. By the time she met them she was ready, eyes blazing, jaw set, to correct a difficult situation.

There was much to set aright. On her arrival, Marge
found that there were no transcripts of previous school records
on any of the children. Many youngsters had chosen
their own classes, without proper guidance. No records were
being kept, no attendance tabulated. It wasn't surprising that
the school had no accreditation. How do you get accreditation
for a school whose existence, until August of 1945, was not
even known? Clearly, Marge had a huge job to do. She succeeded admirably and even obtained accreditation for the
school. She inaugurated a compulsory Saturday school for
children who were disciplinary problems. School attendance
improved as did student discipline. Marge made many curriculum changes. Not surprisingly, she stepped on many toes
along the way. Though feared, she was respected on the hill
and many parents were sincerely grateful to her.

While planning for my mother's visit, I hit on the happy
idea of contacting Margery Crouch. I was looking for a friend
for my mother, someone with a little more maturity than I
had. Marge was older than the wives on the hill. Maybe even
forty! I, too, was impressed with this determined lady and her
missionary zeal. What's more, she was good company as her
never-ending tales of woe concerning the school never failed
to have a humorous twist. She lived alone, unhampered by
husband or children, which meant she had *time*! I thought
that she and Mother would get along well with each other.
Marge was delighted to hear that my mother was coming up
and contacted her during a brief visit to San Francisco during
the winter school vacation. As a result they were already
acquainted before my mother arrived at Los Alamos.

Babes in Arms

Like Margery Crouch, Mom also arrived on the hill eyes
blazing, jaws set, and initially charged with similar missionary
zeal. She too had a big job to do, to fatten up her Phyllis

(her lifetime ambition), to help with her grandson Bobby, to take over when I went to the hospital, and to solace Lee when the anticipated daughter was born. Bring on your water in buckets; bring on your snowstorms! Whatever Los Alamos presented, she was ready for—almost!

Maybe I had better explain about the "anticipated daughter." Somehow, or was I just imagining it, Mom seemed very positive that I would have a girl. She felt sorry for Lee, who seemed to be expecting a boy. Where did I get this idea? Well, she and Dad had sent Christmas-Hannukah presents to all of us. The gifts included a bathrobe for me, a jacket for Lee, a bathrobe for Bobby, and a nice *pink* sweater for little "Hoo." In my letter of thanks for the gifts I wrote:

> . . . and Hoo thinks you think she's a girl by the color
> of the darling sweater you sent her/him.

Mom had last seen Bobby as the toddler who had locked himself in the bathroom at the apartment in San Francisco on the day of Shirley and Bob's wedding. On her arrival at our small cottage, she found to her great delight that her little grandson spoke fluently, took to her immediately and wanted her company constantly. She read to him and Bobby "read" stories right back to her. Bobby, my mother's first grand-child, was a great success.

The commissary impressed Mom. What it lacked in esthetic appeal it more than compensated for in availability of supplies. Ecstatically, she wrote to Dad that there was "mayonnaise, toilet paper and kleenex" for sale at the store, which seemed to her like riches galore. She explored the PX and found irons and other articles that had disappeared from the civilian stores of the outside world years ago. She also found that some products not available at our stores were available in San Francisco.

She marvelled at the scenery as she surveyed the surround-ings from our high mesa. However, the altitude affected her the first few days after her arrival. The smallest effort left her out of breath, and a constant headache plagued her. But a good look at me revived her spirits. Knowing my tendency to gloss over troubles, she had expected to find me worn, exhausted, and generally feeling poorly. Instead, she found me surprisingly healthy.

Then, too, the house wasn't so bad. The one space heater in the hall kept us fairly warm, most of the time. She slept on the living room couch, which made up into a pretty adequate bed. The kitchen was workable except for the kerosene stove, which completely defeated her. When liquids boiled over, and they boiled in no time at all at our high altitude, black smoke coiled up to the ceiling. She was appalled! At its rear, our tiny little oven burned food, yet left food raw up front near its poorly insulated door. One had to remember to constantly rotate food, but one often forgot!

My mother loved our friends at once and quickly became everyone's "Mom." She was quite a rarity. The only other mother of an adult on the hill was Mrs. Hirschfelder, the mother of a well-known theoretical chemist. Mom quickly found Margery Crouch and made plans to see her. She began to relax and enjoy living with us on the hill.

On January 11, just three days after her arrival, I started having labor pains, pains that didn't seem to be getting anywhere. I persuaded Lee and Mom to take a drive with me, not far, just up to a promontory with a lovely view. We made the short drive, with my mother looking apprehensively at me all way. On our return, we had dinner and went to bed. Not until 4:00 A.M. did I get up and go with Lee to the hospital. And even then I simply took forever to produce our baby. Lee slept little, kept me company as much as the hospital staff would let him, got to work when he could, got home to Bobby and Mom as much as possible. The Army hospital rules had lagged behind the many liberalized regulations on the hill. There were no provisions for my mother to get into the hospital and see me. She tried. They wouldn't let her in. So she just stayed home and worried. Finally our second baby, a tiny, perfect *boy* was born in the early morning hours of January 13. I was exhausted; so were Lee and Mom!

But Lee was delighted! A boy, how perfect! Mom would just have to wait a little longer for her granddaughter. We wanted to phone my father at once and tell him the great news. There was no way to make an outside long distance call from the hospital. Lee finally went out into the snow to a pay phone near the commissary, the one we always used, sometimes after waiting in line, to make outside calls. Unable to reach Dad, he telegrammed: BABY BOY BORN PHYLLIS FINE NAME INDEFINITE. We loved the telegram we got back from Dad, which read: DEAR INDEFINITE WELCOME TO THE FAMILY.

Bobby was thrilled with his new brother. He climbed on a large box outside my window and squealed with delight when I held up the baby for him to see. Soon he was off racing around the mesa and shouting to anyone in sight, "I got a new baby. I'm going to *hold* it!" My pregnancy had been broadcast by the doctors at the post. Bobby took care of disseminating information about the birth so, once again, we needed no announcement system.

One luxury available at Los Alamos was maternity care. The medical staff generously allowed us to stay in the hospital for ten gloriously restful days. That wonderful boon was granted despite the fact that the hospital staff was doing its very best to deal simultaneously with the baby boom and the water shortage. The maternity ward was like a club with a very exclusive membership, but a club with a difference.

The water shortage made the difference and necessitated drastic changes in the hospital routine. For example, our food came to us on soft, absorbent paper (not plasticized) plates. Every morning we had fried eggs for breakfast served on one of those blotter-like plates. A challenge to start the day! Toilets could only be flushed twice a day and four new mothers shared a bathroom. Babies were covered somehow with paper towels as we couldn't use cloth diapers, which would need laundering.

Still, I enjoyed my vacation in the hospital and the rest and attention that went with it. Everyday I held court at my window, and chatted with visitors. In fact, the day after our baby was born, I had the distinction of entertaining four SEDs through the window while sitting in bed on a bedpan and listening to the nurses laughing in the hall. "Indefinite" quickly became Larry and more formally Lawrence. And Larry and his new little associates nursed and slept contentedly while we mothers exchanged gems of expertise and freely gave advice all around. We even had time to read the newspaper. Amazing!

Together we caught up with activities in the outside world. Together we shared our hopes and our fears: hopes that a fragile peace could be maintained, and fears that these babies would never know a world committed to solving international problems peacefully. I felt a brief but meaningful respite from my anxieties as I learned of a movement afoot at Los Alamos and at the other atomic sites to do something about regulating the future of the bomb.

Babes in Washington

Ominous news had been coming out of Washington for months. Maybe we shouldn't have been so surprised at the turn of events. Atomic bombs were now a reality, not a theory. Throughout the country there was a growing atmosphere of fear rather than hope. The real significance of nuclear weaponry was beginning to be understood and consequently feared by the citizenry. Little wonder. Newspapers mapped areas in large cities to indicate the potential swath of destruction of an atomic bomb in an imaginary attack, and an anxious public read the newspapers and worried.

A powerful movement was under way to keep nuclear weapons research under military control. Los Alamos as well as Oak Ridge and Hanford could be destined to remain military posts. This movement found its champion in Congressman Andrew May, chairman of the House Military Affairs committee, who cosponsored a bill with Senator Edwin Johnson. The bill itself, drafted in the War Department, appeared innocent enough. The problem was that it contained nothing specific as to the amount or lack of military control and was worded in such a way that military control of nuclear research could continue. All sources of nuclear energy, all related research and production, were to be under control of a commission appointed by the president with the approval of the senate. Appointees could be removed by the president with no explanation given. What was alarming was that it was being rushed through hearings with practically no opportunity for scientists to give their opinions.

In the maternity ward, we wondered what sort of civilians would be willing to work on a military post in peacetime. How could peacetime use of nuclear energy develop? How could civilian scientists, who had a deep commitment to the unwritten code of open exchange of ideas, submit to continued military control? Who were the *military* scientists who could bring projects to fruition? What would happen to the free flow of ideas, without which scientific advances would be severely hampered? What was happening to our dreams of sharing information and of internationalizing the bomb? Was it feasible to turn the bomb over to the infant United Nations? And why were our leaders on the hill so silent?

Oppenheimer was in Washington. We read with interest and pride about his speeches in public forums everywhere. He seemed to be working as a one-man committee to publicize the bomb's message to an ignorant world. He was saying a good deal. He tried to convince senators that scientific "gossip" is the lifeblood of the physicist. He was consulted by the War Department and by the Executive Office. The press followed him on the correct assumption that every word he uttered was newsworthy.

But more needed to be done. Oppenheimer was lecturing as do some professors, believing that informed persons will make the right decisions. Thus he limited his discourses to scientific enlightenment, and left legislation to the legislators. Reportedly, Oppenheimer felt it was useless to try in any other way to prevent the passage of the May-Johnson bill or to prevent military control of the "bomb." Leave science to scientists, and politics to politicians, he cautioned. He sounded discouraged, defeated, wary.

General Groves, too, was speaking in public whenever the occasion presented itself. His general theme was that it would take Russia twenty years to develop a nuclear bomb. (How wrong he was!) He concurred with the growing state of congressional alarm. It was best, he felt, to continue to keep scientists behind barbed wire (how could you?), or technical information would leak out.

(Classified information had leaked out already, but none of us knew it as yet. Klaus Fuchs, a theoretical physicist from the British Mission, had seen to that. A quiet, kind, gentle and well-liked bachelor, he had worked assiduously in the tech area, attended meetings, participated in discussions, observed and learned well—and passed on information to the Soviet Union. Another, David Greenglass, an SED who had worked in the tech area as a machinist, collected information and relayed it to Harry Gold, information that reportedly found its way to the Soviet Union.)

"Lost Almost"

As we, at leisure in the maternity ward, talked about this situation, we recalled with some dismay the political inaction on the hill throughout the previous year. Before Trinity, the

the scientists on the hill with few exceptions had been completely engrossed with the job at hand. There seemed to be little space in their minds for politics. Consequently, there was little talk about the use of the weapon before it was a reality. A few individuals on the hill had made an effort to face a future in which the consequences of the bomb surpassed the imagination. In the spring of 1945, Niels Bohr had written a letter to President Roosevelt recommending that all nuclear information be made available internationally as soon as hostilities were over as the best insurance of peace. Roosevelt died soon after without answering the letter. Also in the spring of 1945, Robert Wilson called a meeting at Los Alamos to try to start serious consideration of the impact of the "gadget." The meeting was held but future meetings were discouraged by Oppenheimer, who felt that mixing science and politics was not appropriate.

At this time, in contrast, at other Manhattan Project sites, notably at the Chicago labs, petitions were signed recommending use of the bomb only after a warning, and only over an unpopulated target. An attempt made to circulate that petition at Los Alamos met with opposition from Oppenheimer. Ironically, the petitions sent from Chicago and from Oak Ridge, were not seen by President Truman.

After the Trinity detonation there was talk on the hill of nothing but the bomb, but no concerted action to control its use. Later in August, after Hiroshima and Nagasaki were demolished, an association concerned with the future of the bomb was formed on the hill and suitably named the Association of Los Alamos Scientists, or ALAS for short. Leon, who attended that meeting, told me that Edward Teller was present and spoke passionately about the necessity of sharing all knowledge of atomic weapons internationally.

As the weather grew colder, bitter jokes abounded on the hill. Some, for example, began calling Los Alamos, "Lost Almost." Some felt at the time that the acronym ALAS was uncomfortably fitting, spelling out our feelings only too well.

But there was among us a group of young scientists who, looking towards the future, felt that there was a fight to be fought and perhaps even to be won. Specifically, the fight was to free atomic research from threatened continued military control. Many young scientists participated in this movement.

The group was headed by Willie Higginbotham, a young man who looked like anything but a fighter as he peered shyly through thick glasses. He was a well-known and loved figure on our hill. Willie came "alive" at musical events on the hill, particularly at square dances. Armed with his accordion and possessing a fabulous knowledge of every dance and song ever composed, as well as a great sense of rhythm, Willie had become our "Mr. Music." He also had been one of the three remaining tenors in the "Messiah" performance and had sung the tenor solos.

As soon as the war was over, Willie and his beloved accordion headed for Washington. He seemed almost like the fabled Don Quixote. He knew nothing of politics or the machinations of government. He seemed innocent and vulnerable, but our Willie and the transient group that followed him to Washington seemed to us to accomplish miracles.

As we tended our babies in the hospital, we read of the exploits of Willie and the young scientists in Washington. These men were taken seriously enough to be given exposure in the press. To hardened reporters, this young group looked more like college sophomores than like scientists. They certainly bore no resemblance to politicians. According to an article in *Newsweek* (Dec. 3, 1945, vol. XXVI, p. 42), eagerly passed around our "Maternity Country Club," this group "knew as much about politics as congressmen knew about nuclear physics." The statement was probably true both ways. The article pointed out that these "babes in Washington" controlled no bloc of votes. What kind of deals could they make? Their ages ranged from twenty-five to thirty-five or -six. Just kids.

Obviously, they lacked political know-how. They were

disorganized and perhaps naive, but they more than compensated for their inexperience with their untiring and
energetic activities and their clear-eyed honesty. Of course,
they were not looking for any "deal." They only wanted to
block the passage of the May-Johnson bill in Congress.
Crowded into a small office with no staff or decent funding,
they worked without salary. They would speak anywhere, at
hospitals, clubs, churches, anywhere. They would buttonhole
congressmen, any congressman. It was strangely comforting
to read about the exploits of these idealistic young men. And,
it was an education to follow their activities.

Another Education

Meanwhile, up on our hill another education was in progress.
While we in the "Maternity Club House" were learning
about the Washington scene, my mother was learning about
Los Alamos. Marge Crouch invited Mom to a "big event" on
the hill, the high school graduation ceremony. Mom was
thrilled to get away from primitive housekeeping and to
attend this community function. Surely enough, she found a
large room full of people, maybe twenty-five or thirty in all,
present for the scheduled event. There were several teachers,
some parents, some students and exactly one graduate! This
sole honoree was the son of a man who had been an employee
of the original Los Alamos Ranch School, which had predated
our community on the hill. The family had stayed on when
the facility changed over to a military-scientific project.

As the principal of the high school, Marge Crouch wanted
to preside over a suitably impressive event. It was, so I hear,
an unusual event in an odd sort of way. The formal address
for the occasion was given by no less than the commanding
officer of our military post. I learned from Mom and from
others that the colonel spoke long and eloquently about his
two and one-half years of service in India. While children

squirmed and whispered and squirmed some more, the inappropriate travelogue went on. What did India with its Taj Mahal, its poverty and heat, have to do with graduation? Once again, in its own inimitable way, the Army had come through. Marge, the embarrassed school principal, was soon at work looking for a more suitable speaker for the next graduation ceremony.

When my stay at the maternity country club ended, tiny Larry and I headed home with a tired Leon through a severe dust storm. We were met at the door by a grimy but radiant Bobby, who now looked enormous to me. As soon as I was in the house, he got his wish; he held his baby brother!

Although I found an eager Bobby, I found a swamped, exhausted Mom. The dust was more than my efficient, meticulous mother could handle. The air was grey, the wind howled, and the dust and sand were sifting through the windows of our loosely assembled little house. I helpfully suggested taping the windows. They responded grimly that they would have used tape gladly if any were available. But there was none to be had anywhere on the hill. Then I learned that the oil heater had failed again the previous evening and that they had just spent a miserable night fighting filthy smoke in subfreezing temperatures. I was the only rested one in the family. But not for long! It was apparent at once that my country club existence was over.

Larry was such a good baby—maybe too good. He never cried. He slept hours between feedings. He seemed so content. Too content? I began to worry about him. Was he eating enough? Was he gaining enough? Why did he sleep so long? Was something wrong? The pediatrician had assured me that I had nothing to worry about; still, I worried.

But what fun it was to see Bobby glowing with delight over his new brother. While I fed Larry, Bobby gave his "bunny" a bottle. One afternoon I found that Bobby had left a cookie in the bassinette for Larry. Where was the jealousy I had expected? Maybe later? I seemed to be worrying about everything. As I usually did, I tried to convince myself that everything was all right—the babies, the family, the world. Any small remaining problems as to the future of nuclear research could be left to Willie and his co-hopefuls. Relax Phyllis and enjoy your children. Try and relax!

Marge invited Mom to go with her on a trip to Taos Pueblo, and the two women headed off for adventure in Marge's beat-up car. On her return, Lee and I bundled up the baby and got Bobby into a snowsuit and off we all went in our grey, desert-damaged model to visit the nearby ancient ruins of the Santa Clara Indians. The Puye Ruins are on a mesa, or more accurately a potrero north of the area. We had learned that the Santa Clara Indians had made that flat, high promontory their home until about three hundred years ago when for some reason they moved their entire community to the valley below.

From the parking area at Puye there is a short climb to the remains of cave dwellings, remnants of the homes these Indians occupied several centuries ago. It was a brilliantly clear day. Snow-covered peaks glowed in the distance. The air was exhilarating. But as I climbed, I began to feel ill and finally I suggested that Lee, Bobby, and Mom go on without me. I settled down in a sheltered spot with Larry and awaited their return.

Larry, serene and content inside a pile of assorted blankets, seemed so trusting. The view before me was breathtaking. Spread before me was a seemingly eternal land untouched by time and uncontaminated by human contact. As my family explored the ruins of an ancient Indian civilization, I thought of other ruins, past and future. I couldn't forget that just over the mountains to the south lay another tongue of land where a weapon had been produced that challenged the assumption that anything on earth could be "eternal."

How ironic that with a new little life in my arms, I was thinking of extinction. My thoughts raced through time. The fossils tell us of forms of life wiped out. Why? What sort of catastrophe hastened their end? What happened to the trilobites? Where have the dinosaurs gone? The earth has at times grown warmer, at times colder. Earthquakes and typhoons cause great damage. But the human race is intelligent, resourceful, and creative, and can survive natural disasters. Would we be intelligent, resourceful, and creative enough to prevent our own annihilation? I doubted it. We can only do ourselves in, I reasoned, and concluded despairingly that we now have the means to do so.

Why did I keep thinking like that? Why couldn't I just enjoy the scene? I hugged Larry close to me and fought back tears as my little family of hikers returned to collect me and our baby and start the drive back to our hill. Fortunately, apart from a feeling of exhaustion, I seemed to be no worse from the experience on our return to "Lost Almost."

10. *On Our Own*

Risky Ventures

SOON IT WAS TIME FOR MY MOTHER to leave our hill and return to San Francisco and to Dad. We were sorry to see her go, sorry Dad hadn't been able to clear the time to come, and, at the same time, glad to be our own family once again. And I wrote to Mom soon after her return:

We hated leaving you in Santa Fe and tried to prolong the evening as long as possible. Consuelo (our baby-sitter) was tired when we returned. Bobby had been blue and noncommunicative with her for about a half-hour. Larry ate, burped and slept as usual, and had just been fed when we returned at close to midnight.

Bobby keeps asking about you, Mom, and insists that you are momentarily expected back "with a train and Grandpa." (Dad, did you note the sequence?) He is very sure of it, and when I tell him he is wrong, he says, "You're a bad girl, Mommy." It's too bad, Bobby and I agree, that our visits with you have to be so short, so intense, so rare, and so suddenly and completely over.

And speaking of Bobby, you'll be interested in his first nursery school report. His teacher finds him "eager, animated, even-tempered," but adds that he is "adamant in his refusal to put on his galoshes." Refusal, my eye! He isn't three yet. He *can't* get them on! *I* can hardly get them on over his shoes! He's never been adamant about anything yet, and I know him pretty well. How can she insist on his doing something he can't do yet?

Remember Tonita who helps us with cleaning? Well, she was all giggles today. She had just arrived on the hill with Juanita (another girl who works in the houses), who met you at the commissary. Tonita reported that Juanita told her, to quote, "Mrs. Fisher's mother is so pretty, that I think men still flirt with her!" Now, what do you think of that?

[Besides being irritable] I was feeling crampy and went to see Dr. Stout the other day. All is OK, although I'm not as far along as I should be. He asked me several questions about what I had been doing. Finally, we got to the Puye trip. He wanted to know some details about the trip. I supplied more information. Suddenly he lashed out, "You little fool! You get maid service and then climb mountains!" He made me feel pretty stupid, and then I realized none of the three of us even considered the possibility that the Puye trip would be too much exertion for me. Anyway, I am all right. He said I was luckier than I deserved to be. Guess he's right.

The days were lengthening. My letters home were full of my delight with Larry as well as with my continuing difficulties of coping with the weather. After one particularly severe dust storm, I wrote the following:

We just dug ourselves out of the worst dust storm to have hit these parts in years and years and years. I could *see* the darn stuff blowing *through* the windows. We were all coughing. Once, I put Larry on the bathinette to change him and played with him there a while. When I picked him up, I could see the outline (in dust) of his little body on the towel, and that although I had adhesive tape around the window! But this particular storm is over. With the help of Tonita, lots of work on my part, and assistance by Leon, we're finally clean again!

While she helped me, Tonita, looking pale and anxious,

told me of her plans to leave the area. She explained that several years ago she had married an "Anglo."

He tried often to encourage her to go with him to his home in Cleveland, but she was afraid to venture far from her home in Tesuque Pueblo. Finally, he left her with three little ones and returned to Cleveland. Then he did a stretch of time with Uncle Sam (in the Army), subsequently returning to his Tonita at Tesuque Pueblo. Tonita has finally agreed to go with him to Cleveland, although she is frightened almost to death at the thought of doing so. I gave her a hug and told her to keep in touch. I want to know what happens to her. Her life has been so limited. How will she adjust to the city away from the only life-style she knows?

I was having a hard enough time adjusting to my new world. I wondered if the move from Tesuque Pueblo to Cleveland would be more difficult for Tonita than had been my move from San Francisco to Albuquerque to Los Alamos. I was afraid it would be.

As a challenge to my adjustment, electrical power shortages continued to plague the community. The solution to ration power, which had now been in effect for a few months, was anything but satisfactory, but no one could come up with a better idea. One half of the residences on the mesa continued to get electric power for the first half of each hour. Then for the next thirty minutes the power supplied the other half of the mesa. The novelty of the situation had worn off. Grudgingly, we continued to accommodate ourselves to alternate half-hours of current and noncurrent. One had to plan carefully. At best it was a challenge, at times a real aggravation. My friends on the project helped make the adjustment smoother.

Louise had her baby around the end of January, and a couple of weeks later Mary had hers. Incredibly we five friends, Rhuby Jean and Minnie included, all have produced babies within a few months' time. You'd almost suspect we got together and planned it that way. Our little corner of "McKeeville" had turned into one giant nursery. With five new babies and five toddlers, our world was full of, as Louise put it, "diapers, training pants, burps, and baby talk."

All five new mothers were glowing. In this strange locale where the scientists had produced their miraculous achievements, we had produced our own little "miracles." For the next weeks we helped one another, took turns shopping, and tended each other's babies.

In some parts of the tech area, scientists were marking time. Meanwhile, in Congress the future of the project was being debated. Now that we were the relieved possessors of two newly recapped tires, we found opportunities on weekends to explore the picturesque area around us by car. And so I wrote:

This March has come in like a LAMB! We've had sunny, bright days and cloudless skies. Saturday morning we scrambled out of the house at around nine o'clock in the morning. We cut across the valley [by car] and climbed up into the Sangre de Cristo mountain range—up past Chimayo, a charming little town, and beyond it to Truchas, a fascinating little village way up towards snow-covered Truchas Peak. There can't be more than a couple of hundred residents there.

Truchas is a hilly, alpine settlement. We found a few tiny houses around a miniature plaza. A few goats, a few sheep, and some sad-looking horses completed the picture. It was like a town out of the past. In fact, it *is* a town still in the past. The people here are Penitentes. They are descendants of the early Spanish Conquistadores. They still speak a Castilian Spanish quite similar to that which their ancestors spoke when they came to the "New World" over three hundred years ago. This Spanish is different in sound as well as in vocabulary from the Mexican-Spanish dialect one hears in this general area.

We were told that they practice an ancient form of Catholicism that involves some painful customs. Every Easter, I'm told, they have a procession to a hill. They carry huge crosses, and whip themselves or one another as they progress to their destination. There someone is selected to "play" the role of Jesus and is suspended for a while on a huge cross. Strangers to the area have tried to witness and photograph this strange procession. Rumors abound as to what has happened to these strangers. We had been warned to ask no questions of anyone at Truchas and not to expect a friendly reception there. So we sur-veyed the idyllic scene before us, let Bobby pet a friendly lamb, contrasted the gentle beauty around us with the stories we had heard, and then quickly moved on.

We continued north, along a mountain road (hurrah for our tires!) to a piny ridge. Here we refrigerated Larry's bottles in the snow and built a piñon fire to warm a bottle in an empty pineapple juice can filled with snow. In the late afternoon, as the sun dropped low over haze from Los Alamos, visible to our western view, we continued on to Dixon, a tiny town, where the now almost invisible mountain road meets the so-called "highway" from Taos. Then, home again in time for a late dinner at the cafeteria.

At the cafeteria that night, we met an effusive, glowing Luis Alvarez, the leader of Leon's group during the war period. Luis, who is about thirty-four or so, told us that he has just been promoted to the rank of full professor at U.C. [University of California], an amazing achievement! He's proud as punch. We were delighted, too.

Another weekend had its own thrills, but of a different sort.

We went skiing last week and I just loved it. Lee is pretty good at skiing, except for stopping—then he just sits. Well, I'm proud to say, I went down gentle slopes and didn't have a single spill, though once I went gracefully through a group of children at the bottom of the hill, scattering them artistically all over the place, because I also couldn't stop or turn and my skis just took me there. We went with the Seeleys. Rhuby Jean and I alternated caring for the two run-abouts and two babies. Lee and Leslie skied most of the time. It was great! We'll do it soon again.

On still another weekend:

We drove to Puye and beyond today. Remember Puye, Mom? This was the wildest ride we have taken yet. Beyond Puye is the crooked chasm of the Santa Clara Canyon. The road goes straight up, almost, then straight down, almost, turns on a dime, almost, and is nicely splattered with boulders along the way. Bobby picked the spot for our picnic, a lovely area way up the canyon, affording a spectacular view of jagged rocks and cliffs with patches of snow all around us. So again we had refrigeration and water for cooking and a nice sunny spot in the pines. We all got sunburned, including Larry. We thought we had our small rascal covered, but he exposed one little arm, which is now a bright pink. Now, we're home, fed, and half of us are in bed. The other half are studying and writing letters. That last mentioned quarter now has to make some baby formula. So, here I go.

Violence

March brought some beautiful weather and several storms. It also brought us our first experience with violence. Our little Bobby was the unfortunate victim. And so I wrote:

Wow! Did Bobby have a bad experience the other day!
He had been playing outside with Jamie and under Mary's
watchful eye. He was happily swinging on a swing suspended from the clothesline next to the "P's" house.
Apparently, Mr. P called to him to get off "their" swing
and Bobby didn't obey. So, Papa P gave Bobby a real
beating. Mary, steaming with rage, brought Bobby home
and told me what had happened. I was so furious I couldn't
speak! Lee went over and learned that, in Mr. P's self-
righteous opinion, this is the only way to properly "discipline" children. His own little boy is so timid that he is
afraid of his own shadow, and no wonder.

Lee really handled the thing quite well and didn't lose
his temper; I would have! Lee got Mr. P to promise to
confine his whipping to his own children. We still weren't
satisfied. What about their poor little child? Moreover, we
have heard that Bobby isn't the only child who has had the
privilege of Mr. P's superior form of training. Lee reported
the incident to the Town Council and learned that Mr. P
had been reported to the Military Police for abusing children several times before. All the military did was send out
an MP who said, "No, No!" The chairman of the Town
Council is a friend of Lee's and works with him at South
Mesa. I'd like to have him [Mr. P] reported to the SPCC
(Society for the Prevention of Cruelty to Children), but
there is no such organization here. In fact, as you know,
there are no services of any kind. No one here has any
authority to stop him or to help the family in any way. The
only solution is to get Mr. P removed from the hill. It's
serious business. Now our Bobby has been so depressed
and seems almost shriveled up. He talks often about "that
bad man." I encourage him to talk about it. I hope I'm
doing the right thing.

While I had been worrying about nuclear violence, now a
real possibility in the outside world, our little Bobby had

experienced some old-fashioned violence right in our "safe" neighborhood. How could I protect him from the ill-tempered acts of mankind as he grew up? How could I reinforce his confidence that people were basically good and kind, a confidence I was losing? What is "good?" What is "kind?" What is "evil?" I had seen good people, with the best of intentions, create a weapon that potentially can dwarf any savagery the world had ever experienced. Was this neighborhood experience to be Bobby's initiation into the realities of the outside world?

Farewells

Perhaps the Town Council had been effective, for about a week later, and to the neighborhood's relief, the Ps suddenly left the hill. A huge Army truck backed up to their house. Hurriedly their possessions were assembled, some in old cartons, and everything was rushed into the waiting truck. Mr. P was nowhere to be seen. Mrs. P, looking haggard and worn, stood disconsolately on the road, watching the men loading her possessions. Her little boy was looking frightened as he had often before.

I offered to watch Warren while Mrs. P supervised the packing, but the offer was not accepted. I asked her to come in and have coffee with me before she left, which she did. Warren played with his hot chocolate and asked over and over for Bobby, who was at nursery school. Mrs. P said nothing about the reason for her leaving so suddenly. Nor did she give me any clue as to the whereabouts of her husband. She felt bitter about her stay at Los Alamos. She made it clear that, in her opinion, her neighbors, including me, hadn't been friendly. She had worked in the tech area, where she had also felt lonely and isolated. She had absolutely no regrets about leaving.

She thanked me for the coffee and chocolate and started to

leave. And that was when I noticed that the movers in their zeal had included the P's garbage can with the collection of boxes and suitcases they had packed. That garbage can was full of garbage! "They took along your garbage!" I called after her. She grabbed her child, ran to the car and drove off to find them if she could. "Oh, hell!" was the last thing I heard her say. Poor, unhappy woman. It looked to me as though the "garbage" of Los Alamos would follow her wherever she was going. And the flavor of our encounter with the Ps was not going to disappear with their removal from the hill, for Bobby continued to show evidence of his experience with her ill-tempered husband, and I wrote:

The neighbors were about to organize to get the the Ps off the hill at the time we learned that they were leaving. Bobby is still a little shy with strangers since his whipping. He did go back to nursery school a few days later, though. But, darn it, he's very, very slow now to warm up to adults. He has had a few nightmares about that "bad man," but seems to be forgetting it finally. Maybe that's why Bobby had been spending more time "playing Larry."

The SEDs were being discharged from the Army. However, as many were university students and most would be returning to their classes scheduled for the next academic year, which would begin in the fall, some of them opted for a few months of continued employment at Los Alamos as civilians. On March 19, I wrote:

Zip, and another day went by! Chuck dropped in by surprise just as we were about to eat dinner, so he joined us. He is a civilian now and has just returned from discharge and a wonderful visit home. He looks handsome in civilian clothes, but that is the only civilian thing about him. He goes back to the barracks, as there is no housing available. He will eat in the mess hall, so it really isn't a

very great change. Betty, his wife, is coming out in June
and will stay for the summer. Murray is east now and will
return soon as a civilian.

We learned about this time that the status of Los Alamos
itself was still unclear. Our little group in Washington was
working hard, but there was still a real possibility that the
project would remain a military installation. My letter
reflected the concern about the future of Los Alamos, a concern which was felt all over the hill.

We're all pretty worried over the possibility of passage
of the May-Johnson bill now in Congress. We'll all be
scared to breathe if the darn thing passes. Under that bill,
I understand, if the military wants to, they can take scientists out of other jobs and make them work on war
research. Every scientist here is praying that it won't
pass. They think that this could mean not only the end of
freedom of research, but possibly the end of democracy as
we know it, and I agree.

Our neighbors, Louise and Brad, were making plans to
leave the hill. This couple was really an enigma to us. As
we watched them prepare to leave, we experienced mixed
feelings. They had been the delight and the mystery of our
little area on the mesa. I described Brad previously as the
pipe-smoking seer who knew everything that was going on
in the labs and out on the sites. After the war was over and
Lee and I could talk more freely, among the things he
straightened out for me was my misconception of the role of
Brad at Los Alamos. Brad, it turned out, was an expediter, a
man who brought needed equipment to the various sites upon
request. He was often where things were "happening" because equipment was needed there. He relayed this information to Louise, who was only too happy to share it with
her willingly gullible audience.

Brad and Louise left Los Alamos and moved to Los Angeles. In a short time, a series of articles appeared in the *Los Angeles Times* under the by-line of our ex-neighbor. The articles were a simplification of the Smyth Report. Apparently they were well received, for in no time Brad was busy working on a documentary film released by MGM under the title "The Beginning or the End." We saw the film. It was surprisingly good, and we noted with interest that he was listed as one of the scientific advisers. Clearly, I was not the only one impressed by his profound look, his intense gaze, and his pipe.

But, wait! Have I been fair to this man? Why criticize a man who, without status in the charmed circle of nuclear cognoscenti, simply publicized information about the bomb? In so doing I missed the significance of Brad's contribution.

Looking back afresh, I'm aware of what an intellectual snob I was about one small occurrence in 1946. After all, he was paid to "deliver the goods" to the various sites at Los Alamos. It was true that he kept his eyes and ears open. It was equally true that he relayed bits of information to Louise. But it is also true that he continued to "deliver the goods" to the American people at a time when it was sorely needed. Scientists, who might have been better resource persons at this time, were too busy looking after their own futures in academia.

The Smyth Report was well received by the scientific community. It was an accuraté and well-written treatise but was of absolutely no use to the man in the street. Its reading audience was necessarily limited. It was Brad who took that report and rewrote it in simple language. He broke the information up into small doses, palatable to the general reader, and sold it to the *Los Angeles Times*.

Then, while academics looked to their own futures, Brad spread the word to Hollywood. Does it matter that he lacked scientific credentials? Brad took the initiative. No one else did. While Oppie was lecturing from the podium to credentialed audiences, Brad got things moving. He brought the message to the press and film industry, and through them to the American public. That's expediting at its best!

Stripes Are Back

Throughout the country, universities were rebuilding their eroded departments. Curriculum changes were initiated and new material was incorporated into traditional disciplines as wartime scientific developments were declassified. Now there was exciting new knowledge to share. Students crowded back into the universities, eager to learn. Many were war-weary ex-GIs, older, wiser, and more serious than they had been in their prewar college days. Their educations were supported by GI stipends.

It was a challenging period for faculty, a time of intellectual ferment and growth. For many physicists in 1946, Leon included, there were choices to be made, and all of them looked good.

Leon had several interviews with representatives from industry who had come to Los Alamos to recruit scientists. He had some preliminary talks with university personnel as well, but decided to make no definite plans before attending a meeting of the American Physical Society, which was to be held in Cambridge, Massachusetts, in early May.

The prospect of Leon's attending a meeting was exciting, but he would be going to "proper Boston" looking like a cowboy unless we got him some new clothes. The baggy jacket still hung in the closet, ready, willing, but unable. Now new clothing was a necessity, and we could delay no longer. Full of hope, we headed for Santa Fe but found again that the stores there had nothing that would fit him.

Undaunted, we drove on to Albuquerque. Here an enthusiastic salesman tried to get him to buy a wildly striped suit, the only suit Leon's size in the store. Bobby listened carefully as the eager salesman informed him that he really should purchase that suit because "stripes are back in style again." But Leon, unimpressed by his selling rhetoric, left without making a purchase. Discouraged, we started the long drive back. On the way and on an upgrade, we slowed down behind a huge truck that was raising more than its share of dust. On the rear panel of the truck were brightly painted diagonal stripes (which we could see through the dust, even when when we couldn't see the machine). "Look!" called Bobby in great excitement as he pointed. "The man was right; stripes *are* back!"

Holiday Time on the Hill

Easter was just around the corner. The commissary stocked huge hams for the holiday. Some of the Christians in the community prepared a sunrise service appropriate for the occasion. Down in Santa Fe and in many of the pueblos, plans were under way for suitable festivals. The huge cottonwoods in the valley were displaying bright green buds. This welcome sight and other signs of spring in the valley contributed to the festive spirit all around us.

It was at this time too that the Jewish community at Los Alamos came alive and reserved Fuller Lodge for their Passover Seder, an ancient holiday commemorating the escape of the ancient Jews from slavery in Egypt to freedom in the promised land. The Seder is the service that tells the Passover story. It seemed an especially appropriate celebration in the spring of 1946. In Europe the horrible ovens of Hitler were no longer belching forth smoke, and the Jews who had survived the holocaust could start to rebuild their shattered lives. Many would leave Germany and find a "promised land" somewhere else.

Now with the war over it might be possible locate the traditional food for the dinner that accompanies the service.

As far as I can recall, this was the first communal Jewish event on our hill. We were all excited at the prospect, but how would we arrange the ritual, the proper food, and all that was needed to make the evening appropriately meaningful and enjoyable? Well, we decided to divide the responsibilities. I was asked to make the matzo balls for the soup. This is what I wrote:

What fun! I'm to cook the matzo balls for the big Passover Seder here on the hill. I even practiced making them a few nights ago, and they were voted a big success although they were a little odd. You see, there was no chicken fat to be had anywhere around and I substituted margerine. Tomorrow, we will call Maggidson's, a Jewish delicatessen in Albuquerque, to see if they can send us about a quart of chicken fat in time to make the matzo balls for the Seder.

That was to be a serious undertaking. For matzo balls I needed matzo meal, but where would I find matzo meal? Albuquerque? Fine, Now, matzo balls are always made with chicken fat. I'd need quite a lot. We had checked the area. None could be found in the Santa Fe area, or in Albuquerque. So, at my request, chicken fat as well as matzo meal were ordered from somewhere in Chicago. What's more, I was told that I could have the assistance of a GI who would be given time off from work to help me.

When the great day arrived, an Army jeep pulled up to our little house and unloaded a huge carton of matzo meal and jar after jar of chicken fat. We expected thirty-five or forty guests at the dinner. I had enough supplies to feed hundreds! Then, to my delight, our SED friend, Jim Keck, arrived to help me. He was the GI who had been given time off to be of assistance. We had a wonderful, sticky, greasy time making about 150 matzo balls. We finished our job just as a jeep materialized at our doorstep early in the afternoon.

Our production was loaded into the jeep and taken to Fuller Lodge. Our job was done. A beaming, enthusiastic Jim, who is not Jewish, decided that he was going to attend the dinner as were several other SED friends.

That evening, an expectant crowd gathered at the Lodge. The Seder service was read, old traditional songs were sung (although some of us didn't know the words, and others didn't know the melodies). Then came the anticipated, traditional Passover dinner. Jim looked pleased, and I was excited as the waiters brought in the soup. But, when we tasted it we were appalled. The soup had absolutely *no* taste. Somehow we had missed a step in the planning. The chef in the kitchen had thought all you needed to make matzo ball soup was to boil the matzo balls in water and serve them in the same water. Not at all! They must be served in *chicken soup*! In all our planning, no one had thought to tell the chef that we needed chicken soup. And he, innocent man, must have thought that the concoction he was dishing up was just one of the quaint and interesting traditions of the descendants of a quaint and interesting people. I winced as I recalled my earliest thoughts about the Indians and my first impressions of their "quaint traditions." I had been just as ignorant.

Jim tasted his tasteless soup cautiously as waves of laughter eddied and flowed at the several tables. "Interesting," he commented. As the laughter continued, we all hastened to explain to him how the soup should have been served, and added that this time the SNAFU [acronym for the humorous military slogan: "Situation normal; all fouled up"] was of our own doing.

At the end of the dinner, the chaplain gaveled the participants to silence and commenced to give a sermon, albeit a short one. I don't recall that anyone asked him to speak and remember the impression that the talk was gratuitous. India, once again, supplied the background for a speech. He spoke of the people of India and their reverence for all life, and gave the example of villagers in India existing alongside of maurauding tigers, somehow tying that in to his pleasure in joining us at this feast. It sounded to me as though we were being compared to man-eating tigers! How particularly inappropriate at a time when we were learning to our absolute horror that many millions of our co-religionists had been fed to the beastly ovens of Hitler's Third Reich.

As we left the hall, we could hear different voices asking many questions. Who had asked the chaplain to speak? Had the chaplain had too much to drink? Did he realize what he was saying? We came home to a messy kitchen full of matzo meal and chicken fat, a bedraggled reminder of a dinner that went awry. The next day I purchased cans of chicken soup at the commissary, made loads of matzo balls, and had a crowd in for a corrected first course. That much I could correct. I couldn't undo or redo the chaplain's sermonette.

Our World Widens

The pace of activities on the hill slowed, and the residents of our community continued making various future plans for the next phase of their lives. For our part, we focused on vacation plans before tackling the realities of our ultimate move. Thus I wrote:

> Look, Memorial Day, May 30, is on a Thursday. We figure we could take the following Friday off and also the following Monday and have time for a trip to Grand Canyon. Would you like to meet us there? If so, we could spend four days there and bring Bobby and Larry. That way, we could climb around parts of the canyon and so could you. We could take turns staying with the kiddies. What do you think of that? Pul-lease do it! We could have tons of fun. So could you, and you both are about due a real vacation.

To my delight, my parents were enthusiastic about the idea and made plans to meet us at Grand Canyon. Before we could take this proposed trip, Lee made ready to leave for Boston and the American Physical Society meeting. The necessary suit was finally purchased in Santa Fe, his suitcase was dusted off and packed. Before I knew it, he was off by train to Boston and then to fabulous New York City.

A few days later, during his absence, I sent the following letter home:

I'm feeling OK now, although I fainted night before last after being woozy all day from hitting my head on a kitchen cabinet door. Peggy, Jim, Murray and Chuck took turns keeping me company and taking care of the little ones. Peg stayed over two nights. All that is left now is one swell headache! I'll write more details later. My eyes still won't quite behave.

Later I filled in more details:

I just wrote to my happy, wandering husband. He is having such a wonderful time. He is seeing loads of people he used to know, old classmates, U.C. faculty, etc. He felt privileged to hear Lise Meitner (famous German physicist known for her early work on atomic physcis) address the Physical Society Meeting, and found her talk absolutely fascinating.

But, I've been a first-class pill while he has been away. Actually, indirectly, it was his fault. I was putting some bowls in the lower cabinet and listening to the news on the radio. I heard that there had been a serious train wreck on the route going to Boston. Leon was on a train, on that route at that time. (However, he was not in the train that was derailed.) I jumped up, scared, and banged my head on the upper cabinet door. It almost knocked me out. I lay down for a while; then, feeling better, I went outside to get Larry's buggy. Things started spinning and I sat down on the ground. Lois (a new neighbor) helped me back into the house and put an ice pack on my head, and I felt better. I rested all afternoon and in the evening felt OK. Jim, Murray, Chuck and Peggy all came over to baby-sit, and I went to the last rehearsal of the chorus before our concert scheduled for Friday. That was a mistake. I got dizzier and dizzier at the rehearsal. One of the basses, Dave Judd, noticed me and decided to drive me home. Well, Dave got me just to the door when I pulled a perfect faint. They called the ambulance and I was taken to the hospital. They discovered my head was still there (though not functioning well), plus quite a lump, but that I was really OK. My eyes wouldn't behave, not for a few days. I had a slight concussion. I begged to go home, as Lee was away and I was afraid to leave the babies. Peg offered to stay with me, and Florence, a nurse who lives across the street, was notified to look in on me.

My baby-sitting team was just wonderful. Peg stayed overnight with me. Jim, Chuck, and Murray took shifts staying with me during the day and saw to it that I was never alone. They did dishes, made formula, fed the kiddies, put Bobby on the toilet at night, etc. They were all just wonderful about it. I still have some headache, but last night I felt well enough to take part in the concert.

I continued the letter a few days later:

I just returned from a meeting of the Choral Society where, believe it or not, I was just elected president! It really floored me because I'm about the youngest and one of the least experienced singers in the group. The executive committee is meeting here tomorrow night to plan the program for the summer. It behooves me to make some cookies for tomorrow, don't you think?

Lee will definitely be back Sunday and will arrive at

Lamy at two P.M. I'm planning to drive down with Bobby and Larry to meet him. His trip has been just wonderful. He was delighted with your letter and pleased with the check you sent. And he used it well! He had a wonderful time getting tickets for some great performances and even was lucky enough to hear Marian Anderson on the night he got to New York. He saw "Candida," "Oklahoma," and "The Glass Menagerie." He has been staying at the home of Murray's family. He describes it as a lovely place and, best of all, thinks the world of Murray's parents. He has seen so many of his friends, attended fascinating meetings and, in general, is feeling no pain! He even treated himself to a ride to the top of the Empire State Building. He had been staring up at the building from across the street until a policeman made him stop, as (he was told) it could start everyone staring up and then someone's pocket might be picked or there could be some sort of grim accident.

Lee even found time for a shopping spree and toured Macy's, Bonwit Teller's and Saks. He has been to NYU [New York University] and plans to visit Columbia and Princeton. This is the first traveling he has ever done with time for fun and he is just having a super-splendiferous time of it. And, between you and me, he certainly deserves it!

When I returned from choral rehearsal, I found all asleep except our—notice "our"—cat. It's the little one that was wandering around when you were here, Mom. She had belonged to people who left the hill. Recently she just belonged to the neighborhood. Well, she'd been quite pregnant lately, but that's now past history. She came in and wouldn't leave. Jim and Murray were over. We decided that her kittens must be due. I was elected Dr. Stout (the name of our obstetrician), or rather, Dr. Pleasingly Plump. I officiated and had two excellent assistants for a while. Jim and Murray stuck around until after midnight, but no kittens arrived. Number one arrived at five in the morning. Number two arrived just a little later and didn't survive. Bobby [upon awakening in the morning] was so thrilled to see a brand new baby kitten. However, he proved he doesn't quite have the "facts" down pat. Bonnie asked our little expert where the kitten came from, and he replied, "From the hospital, of course!"

As planned, we met the train at Lamy. We found an excited, animated Leon. He'd been to the big cities and he had loved them. Lee's trip was totally wonderful. The conference really was a thrill. In order to visit New York City, he took three extra days off. So we still have a few days of vacation time left over for Grand Canyon.

In our absence, mommy cat had been busy. On our return we found that, in a box in our kitchen under our semi-operable stove, there are now three little kittens. One is tiger-striped like mommy and two are orange presumably like daddy. I wasn't needed to officiate. Mama cat felt just fine when it was all over. I was deeply impressed with her skill and ability, and more than just a wee bit jealous.

We left our feline family content in their little box, put our two little ones to bed in our box-like house, and then we settled down to discuss the most important result of Leon's trip. He had been offered an assistant professorship in physics at New York University, and he very much wanted to accept that position. I felt overwhelmed. New York is three thousand miles from San Francisco! I had somehow assumed that we would return to the west coast and perhaps even to the Bay Area. Then too, I thought of the cross-hatched streets of New York City, as I had seen them diagrammed in the *New York Times*, and over which had been superimposed drawings of possible Hiroshima-like bomb damage. But through it all came visions of fabulous music halls, great operas, and wonderful museums. How opposite was this picture to the present reality of our life of relative cultural deprivation on an isolated, barren plateau.

We laughed as we reviewed our year and a half on the hill. We recalled a "cultural evening" featuring a violin, cello, and piano trio, at which one of the performers remarked at the close of a selection, "Well! We all ended together!" We remembered the impromptu skits, the very amateur performance of "Arsenic and Old Lace," the records, some pretty scratchy, we all loaned to our local radio station so that we could share classical music. Then we turned on our radio to local station KOB and heard the familiar twang of cowboy music and then imagined the plethora of cultural possibilities that would open up if we made this move to New York.

The move would be easier for Leon than for me. His childhood years had been divided among Montreal, New York and San Francisco. He felt no strong ties to any particular place but savored the challenge of new scenes. I had lived only in San Francisco. When we were finally in bed and an exhausted Leon was sound asleep, I thought of Tonita. She hadn't been able to adjust to Cleveland, to her a strange and totally bewildering place. She had just returned to her pueblo with her children but without her husband. Was I any less provincial than Tonita? How would I do in New York?

I began to realize how much I would miss Los Alamos. As I marveled at the fresh mountain air, the azure skies, the snowy vista across the desert, I knew that soon these would all be very precious memories to store up. I thought of all our friends on the hill who would soon be scattered all over the United States. We had shared so much, learned so much from each other. How would we keep "in touch"? Bobby was thriving in the invigorating atmosphere on our mesa. A relaxed Leon, no longer under pressure, was joyously relating his travel experiences over and over again to everyone who was interested. Even our cat was purring contentedly as she cared for her little family. But in this scene of tranquility, I

felt apprehensive not only about the move but also about my
baby. As I wrote:

> I've been so worried about Larry lately. He hasn't gained
> as much as I wanted [him to]. His complexion has seemed
> grey and he hasn't been as lively as I feel he should be.
> Dr. Love (who has replaced Dr. Barnett) just laughed at
> my worries. But, last week, Larry practically stopped eat-
> ing, though he was as sweet and pleasant as ever. I
> couldn't get more than an ounce or at the most two ounces
> [of formula] down him at a feeding. Larry, at three months
> of age, was averaging about seven or eight ounces a day!
> Again, Dr. Love was just no help, calling it "just a feeding
> problem" and finding no cause for it. Larry's weight had
> dropped from 12 pounds 14 ounces to 11 pounds 10 ounces.
> I was both alarmed and disgusted. I took Larry to see
> Dr. Lathrop, a pediatrician in Santa Fe. He found plenty
> wrong. Larry needs iron and vitamin B. He also has a sore
> throat. The doctor asked me if I had had toxemia when I
> was pregnant and declared that Larry showed the results of
> it. He should have been taking vitamins and iron all along.
> Now I have a nice slimy goo to soothe Larry's throat and
> the needed vitamins and iron. I feel more encouraged.

I wondered, at the time, how much of Larry's difficulties
were related to my continuing anxiety about the new weapons, the fragile peace, our future? How much did my baby
"feel" my tensions? Could I learn to just live each day fully
and let the future take care of itself? The happiness and well-
being of my whole family depended on that.

Humpty Dumpty

An opportunity to check out the effect my tensions had on my
family soon presented itself. A flurry of excitement greeted an

announcement on the hill that a psychiatrist from Oak Ridge, Tennessee, would be visiting our project for a week. Parents of nursery school children were alerted and invited to bring their children in for one diagnostic appointment. I was eager to take advantage of the psychiatrist's brief visit and made an appointment to take Bobby to the hospital to see him.

I was very proud of Bobby and not concerned about him. At the ripe old age of three he was a lively, bright, and interesting little fellow. Then, why should I bring him in for diagnosis? Very probably, I wanted reassurance from the doctor. In fact, I wouldn't have minded at all if the visiting psychiatrist had showered me with praise after interviewing or examining or playing with my super son. I could even imagine the amazed expert saying to me, "Now that's a terrific kid! He's marvelous! How did you do it?"

Up to a point, all went as planned. Bobby spent about forty-five minutes with the doctor. Then I was heralded into his office for a brief summary of his findings. I expected, at the least, a tribute, ecstatic praise and compliments. That isn't what happened.

I was met by a serious-faced man who motioned me silently to a chair. He sat across from me, holding in his hands some of Bobby's drawings. I could see at once that the mood wasn't congratulatory; it was solemn. He asked me if I had any questions. No, I had none. I just wanted to hear his glowing report. None was forthcoming. Instead, he proceeded to tell me that Bobby seemed deceptively happy and well adjusted, but he was indeed struggling with some problems. Carefully, he spread out the drawings.

"You see, Bobby drew a train here," he pointed out, indicating some vague rectangles connected by crooked lines. "Now," he added, "Where does a train go?"

"Away!" he finished for me when I hesitated to answer. "And, look here," he continued. I saw a vague oval. "See this? He called it Humpty Dumpty. What is Humpty Dumpty?"

"An egg," I answered meekly.

"Right! And what happened to Humpty Dumpty?" I felt as though I were taking an oral examination and not doing very well.

"He broke," I mumbled.

The doctor waited for the message to sink in. Then, in a more kindly, fatherly tone, he added, "You see, your son is afraid someone will go out of his life. He also feels life is hazardous. Quite a load for a little three-year-old, don't you think?"

Numbly, I nodded. My time was up. I thanked the doctor and left with Bobby's pictures in my shaking hand. My mind was churning as I picked up my "only apparently happy" child in the waiting room. Perhaps I hadn't realized how much Bobby had picked up my anxieties. Was I making Bobby feel insecure? Did he have to *appear* well put together in order to make *me* happy? What was going on? At a loss for what to think, I sat down on a stump while my son played contentedly (Was he *really* contented?) in the dirt. I looked again at Bobby's art work. Most of it was scribbling, but there they were, those tell-tale forms, over here the connected rectangles, and down there the vague oval.

Suddenly, I felt like laughing. From having observed Bobby and his little contemporaries, I realized that a three-year-old doesn't draw unless he is really precocious artistically, which wasn't true in my son's case. Even then, he draws only what he is taught to draw, and then only if he can master the necessary control. I remembered watching Leon as he carefully taught Bobby to draw a train and a face. As far as I had seen, these were the only things Leon *could* draw. The psychiatrist had asked Bobby to draw something and this little three year old had complied, drawing the only things he had learned. Whew! What a relief!

But, wait a minute! Then, I should be worrying about Leon, not Bobby. Is Leon deceptively cheerful? Is he cheerful? Does Leon want to go away? From me? Does he want

me to go away? Does *he* feel fragile? Is he about to go smash?
Does he think I am about to go smash? Am I? Should I
worry about my husband? Me? Hm.

I showed the drawings to Leon that evening. Highly
amused, he searched through a drawer and found some cancelled checks. On the back of some of them he had drawn a
a train for Bobby. The connected rectangles were in evidence,
only my husband, being more mature, had also drawn wheels
on his trains. Scattered around the train masterpiece, were
several Humpty Dumptys, some smiling, some crying. Leon
had used these simple forms to teach his son everything,
practically everything, he knew about drawing.

After revealing his art work to me, Leon, with a display of
intelligence not available to the doctor or to me that afternoon, pointed out very correctly that trains also come.
Then he summed up the round-robin of concern. First, the
psychiatrist expressed concerned about Bobby; second, I had
transferred that concern, briefly, to Leon. Now, Leon completed the circle with a third interpretation. Possibly, just
possibly, the psychiatrist, while studying the train and the
egg, was interpreting his *own* feeling that life is somewhat
hazardous at the home of the atomic bomb. Perhaps he read,
in these drawings, *his own* desire to leave Los Alamos just as
soon as possible and take the next train back to the relative
sanity and safety of Oak Ridge, Tennessee. In that case, Leon
would cheerfully offer to drive him to the train!

As we laughed over the various interpretations of Bobby's
drawings, we were reminded by the train picture that we
were in the midst of planning to "go away" with our little
ones to Grand Canyon. We had better proceed with our plans
for that trip.

11. *Transients*

BEFORE WE LEFT ON OUR TRIP, news of a second horrifying radiation accident circulated around the hill. On May 21, 1946, Louis Slotin was demonstrating an experiment with a critical assembly. A group of scientists watched as he pushed two parts of a subcritical assembly of plutonium together using only a screwdriver to keep them separated. Suddenly the screwdriver slipped and Slotin was seriously irradiated. He died seven days later. I was at the hospital about the time he died. I had taken Larry to the pediatrician for a checkup. As I walked down the hall I saw a tragic little group leaving Slotin's room. With the doctors was a grief-stricken woman, Slotin's mother, who had been sent for after the seriousness of the accident was appraised. Another scientist in the group that had watched the bomb assembly suffered radiation sickness but recovered. Again, as in the case of Harry Daghlian, it was a sobering lesson. All over the hill, horrified little groups discussed the tragedy.

Soon it was time to put aside, temporarily, our involvement with the oppressive sense of gloom and guilt of Los Alamos. We loaded up our shabby car with all the necessities for the four of us and headed down to Albuquerque. Then we turned west along a two-lane highway that cut an asphalt streak through the empty desert. We followed that slender, dark ribbon all the way through western New Mexico and across Arizona. The air was hot, almost stifling. A "desert bag," a large canvas container, flapped outside our car door, carrying water for us on the trip. I felt a little apprehensive when I

peered out our car windows. I saw parts of abandoned automobiles and mangled tires strewn about at intervals at the
side of the highway. Clearly, some cars had died and dis-
integrated along the way. I fully expected to see vultures
circling in the air above us, waiting for our exhausted little
car to quietly succumb. However, we made it without mishap
to the mountains of Arizona and beyond to the magnificent
Grand Canyon of the Colorado River.

We met my parents there as planned, and stayed with them
for three days at the old and stately El Tovar Hotel, located
almost at the edge of the spectacular Grand Canyon. It was a
great reunion, although our pleasure was somewhat dimin-
ished by their immediate concern over the appearance of our
pale, tiny Larry. He was not a large, vigorous baby like
Bobby had been. And Bobby, talkative and vivacious, was
never separated from his mangy, worn, stained bunny. Mom
couldn't understand why we allowed Bobby to drag such a
disreputable animal around with him. Why couldn't Bobby
love a nice, neat, new one just as well? She had noticed that
there were attractive, stuffed animals for sale right in the
hotel shop. Finally she took matters into her own hands and
bought Bobby a fresh, new bunny. It seemed to work! During
the day, an unconcerned, delighted child played contentedly
with his new possession. Mom was pleased with the success
of her replacement. Later in the day, when she had the
chance, Mom dropped the filthy old bunny into a convenient
wastebasket in the hotel lobby.

Nighttime, however, was a different story. A wailing,
roaring Bobby refused to be comforted. Louder and louder he
cried for his old precious bunny. We were certain that our
son was keeping everyone awake at the hotel. In desperation,
Leon got up and dressed. Wearily, he searched the waste-
baskets of the hotel lobby. No luck. Finally, Leon went outside behind the hotel and found a long row of garbage cans.
Little did it matter that, in the velvety sky above, the stars
shone brightly. He was looking *down*! Grimly, he searched

through the cans until he found the lost bunny, now more shabby than ever. Bunny was cleaned up as well as possible and returned to a grateful Bobby who promptly fell into an exhausted sleep. I imagine that was also true for many other fatigued, irritated guests at that hotel, once the racket in our room ended.

And my embarrassed mother had learned a lesson. So had I. That shabby toy obviously had a very important role in the life of one small child and couldn't be eliminated and replaced so easily. I should have insisted on keeping the old bunny. For the rest of our vacation, the new bunny, so colorful and clean, sat lonesomely on the hotel dresser, reminding me of my poor judgement and remaining completely ignored by Bobby.

The next morning at breakfast, we felt all eyes on us. Our notoriety, however, didn't prevent our enjoying a gargantuan meal. My contrite parents offered to baby-sit for the day. Their offer accepted, Leon and I quickly forgot the miseries of the previous night as we rode on mules down 5,000 feet in altitude to the bottom of the canyon, a spectacular trip. Past canyon walls of brilliant hues we rode as the tiny trail zig-zagged, descending sharply to its lush, tropical floor. There the cool waters of the turbulent Colorado River bathed the feet of two tired riders. After lunch deep in the red-rocked chasm, we climbed back up the steep trail to our hotel at the rim and to our waiting family.

We were glowing with enthusiasm as we tried to describe the glorious sights we had seen on our day-long mule trip, but my parents weren't ready to listen. They had something to tell us. Their long day with Larry had heightened their anxieties. They were actually afraid that Larry was such a delicate baby that he might not survive. He had practically refused his bottle all day long. He hadn't cried; he just lay motionless. They were thoroughly alarmed.

Larry had been eating pretty well for me. He did seem better after my visit to Dr. Lathrop in Santa Fe. I had been feeling more encouraged. Now I began to feel my old sense of panic returning. Maybe, I tried to reassure myself, he was reacting to their concern as he had, in the past, responded to mine. I felt better the next day when Larry took a fair amount of formula when I fed him.

The memory of a thrilling view of an unusual part of the outside world was replaced by worry as we traveled back through the parched desert land. It was a sober ride back to our hill. How serious a problem did we have? Was Larry just a sensitive child? We decided not to trust our own judgment in this matter but to get further medical opinions. (These opinions turned out to be reassuring. After we left Los Alamos, he thrived. He grew into a fine, healthy adult. It's hard for me to remember today how much I used to worry about him.)

Good-bye

Ever since Los Alamos had been a military post, the MPs at the east and west gates had routinely copied down the license plate number of every car entering and leaving the project. Sometime around the end of May of 1946, this task was recognized to be unnecessarily long and laborious, occasionally resulting in the backup of traffic. Then someone had a bright idea: issue Los Alamos license plates! They could be small, have shorter numbers, and be affixed to the regular license plate. Simple!

Consequently, around the beginning of June, the post bulletin carried a new order. Each car was to have a Los Alamos license in addition to the required state license. These local additions were available Monday through Friday at the motor pool. They were to be attached to our licenses by the end of June. I don't remember anyone hastening to comply with the new regulation. Certainly *we* didn't. We had a month in which to make the necessary adjustments, and we had every intention of letting it go until close to the June 30 deadline. Why hurry?

There was a lot to capture and hold our attention during the lengthening summer days of early June. Wartime Los Alamos was literally disappearing before our eyes. As our isolation evaporated, new faces appeared on our hill. Many familiar GIs who had left the hill were sporting new attires when they returned briefly as civilians. The overwhelming military presence was beginning to seem less ubiquitous. The military license plate directive seemed like the last gasp of the old regime. Fairly trivial, nothing important. Good humoredly, we would comply—in time.

Roasting the military had long been one of our favorite indoor sports. Soon we were roasting politicians, too. Continuously following the exploits of our men in Washington, we learned about their impact on congressmen who were studying the May-Johnson bill and considering the future of the atomic energy projects. Senator Brian McMahon had been willing to draft an alternate bill that would leave the future of the projects in civilian hands. Hopefully, we followed the arguments, pro and con, concerning the two proposed bills as they appeared in the *New York Times*. We felt, however, that the material we saw in print was guided more by emotion than by rational consideration. We weren't impressed at all by the level of thinking going on in our nation's capital. And so I wrote:

What do you think of the right honorable Congressman May? Have you read the arguments for and against the May-Johnson bill? We thought it would be interesting to make a study of the IQs of congressmen. Lee suggested that you'd have to add them up to make 100, but now I think you'd have to multiply!

Perhaps we were becoming extremely critical of the outside world in part because we were soon to leave this crazy land

of brilliant color, cliffs and chasms. Where else could we find
an equally colorful community with its artificial mix of military and scientific personnel intermixed with the native
population? We were becoming defensive about Los Alamos
and also a little wary of the outside world. It had been such
an intense experience, and parting was difficult. Some families
on the hill were beginning to pull away emotionally as they
planned their non-Los Alamos futures. There were many
attempts on the hill to celebrate the closeness we had had.
For this purpose, many departments and sections in the labs
held parties and outings. It was in recognition of these
changes that our little choral society, too, decided to have an
outing for its members and their families before they all
separated, probably not to return. Once again, as had been
done for the Passover dinner, the group planned the event in
detail. And so I wrote:

> The choral society will have a picnic Sunday. It won't be
> much work for me (as president) as many of the members
> like responsibility, and they have volunteered to undertake
> most of the planning and preparing. Transportation, food,
> fires, and stick whittling (!) are all under capable chair-
> men. All I have to do is pick up the hot dogs at the com-
> missary and, after our cookout, present "Maestro" Bob
> Dike his gift from a grateful group.

The choristers picked a spot up and over the Jemez mountains directly to our west, past the immense Valle Grande
(the huge crater of an extinct volcano), and down the other
side to a public campsite. Most of them planned to leave
Los Alamos early, drive to the campsite, get fires started and
set up the luncheon. They were to bring rolls, mustard, salad,
fruit and cupcakes. One of the members of our chorus, a
physician, presented a strong case for the following plan. He
pointed out that hot dogs can spoil after a trip in a hot car
and particularly if they are then left in the heat while the

fires are prepared. It would be best, he cautioned, to pick them up as late as possible and bring them to the chosen site at the last minute. We listened respectfully and made plans accordingly. And so it was that the Fishers volunteered to come to the site a little later and bring the hot dogs for the the whole group.

The picnic day in mid-June dawned bright, clear and warm. The group of amateur musicians, leaving early on a Sunday morning, traveled like a convoy out the west gate and snaked up the mountains and over the 9,500-foot pass. Later in the morning, according to our prearranged plan, Leon and I drove with our two little ones to the commissary at exactly ten o'clock. A carton full of hot dogs was ready for us and was loaded into the trunk of our car. Cheerfully we headed towards the west gate. Everything was on schedule. We anticipated no problem. Hah! The Army had one more surprise for us. We were stopped at the west gate by the MPs who told us that we could not leave the hill.

"What's the matter?" asked Leon.

"No one can leave the project without a Los Alamos license plate on his car," was the startling reply.

"But we have until the *end* of the month to put them on!" Leon argued, and added, "This is completely ridiculous!"

"It's not our decision," continued the MP. "We were given orders. We can't let anyone out without those new licenses. Sorry. Regulations."

"Where did the order come from?"

"The Colonel himself!"

"And when?"

"Fifteen minutes ago."

"Fifteen minutes ago? Let me call him!"

"You can't. He isn't here. He was pretty mad. Said not enough people are putting the license plates on. He just came out through the gate. He's gone fishing."

While this conversation was going on, the car was gradually warming up, and so were our tempers. Certainly, the hot dogs were heating nicely in the trunk of the car. Briefly, we considered returning to the so-called center of town, getting plates and affixing same. Quickly we realized that we couldn't get the license plates because the motor pool was securely locked up until Monday. Leon asked to use the MP's phone to locate the military officer who had been left in charge for the day. If located, and if willing, the Officer of the Day could rescind the order. Leon probably made at least ten phone calls. He succeeded in finding out who was in charge, but no one could locate the officer. Finally in desperation, he called a friend and colleague, Leslie Seeley, on the phone. Between the two of them, they figured that the most logical place the major would be on a Sunday morning was in church. At the time of their animated conversation, church services were being held at theater number two. Leslie offered to go to church and try to find the officer and sug-gested that Leon wait at the gate.

We waited in the sun, cooking nicely along with the hot dogs. Leslie went to the church service, hurried down the aisle, fortunately found the major and told him that he was needed for a sort of minor emergency. He accompanied the major to an office to the side of the theater and explained the situation. And fortunately, too, the major responded by contacting the MPs at the gates and countermanding the order.

Finally, we were free to drive up the mountain road behind Los Alamos. As we drove up the winding, bumpy road towards the high mountain pass, we noticed that dark clouds were gathering ominously in the summer sky. We arrived at the selected site in the early afternoon just as a storm broke over the assembled choral group. To anxious queries as to why we were so late, we answered, "You wouldn't believe us if we told you." Hastily the hot dogs were speared on the whittled sticks. Hastily they were distributed and a very brief, wet picinic was "enjoyed" by all as we devoured hot dogs and rolls, gulped down juice or coffee, grabbed cupcakes and fruit, threw Bob Dike his gift (my speech to Bob consisted of "Here! Thanks!"), and fled to our cars. A frantic convoy hastened to drive home before the downpour turned the boulder-strewn, steeply graded dirt road into a wild river of flowing mud.

We made it back safely. Los Alamos was still basking in the summer sun on our return. A beaming Leslie asked a simple question, "How was the picnic?"

"Don't ask!" growled Leon.

Hello

A few days later, a bitter-sweet surprise was in store for me. After shopping at the commissary, I headed for the checkout stand and suddenly was face to face with someone I hadn't seen in ten years. We both were really startled. Her long blonde braids were gone. Gone also was the sparkle from her eyes. To me, she looked worn and tired compared with my memory of the glowing girl I had last seen in high school in 1936. I had a million reactions at once and apparently so did she. And I wrote:

Last week I really had a surprise. I was shopping in the commissary when a girl walked up to me and asked, "Aren't you Phyllis?" I was, and she was—Sigrid! I just about fell over! This is the last place in the world I ever expected to see her! She was completely flustered and so was I. She wrote out a check while talking to me. On one line, she wrote "$15.00" and on the next line, "Twenty dollars" and, instead of endorsing the check on the back, she wrote "Cash." Then she tore it up and started all over again. I invited her to visit me the following week with her two-year-old daughter, Annabel. That evening, when I told Lee about meeting her, for some reason I was so upset that I burst into tears.

Why the tears? Who was Sigrid? As a child, she had come with her mother to the United States from Germany. They lived with a widower, a German doctor, and his two children. Her mother was the housekeeper and surrogate mother for his children. Sigrid and I were classmates in high school and attended the same camp in the summer. I remembered her as a bright, charming girl with a ready smile and even disposition.

She lived in a different part of San Francisco than I did. We didn't visit one another's homes often. One day, I visited Sigrid and, to my horror, found the house full of Nazi literature. On the cover of one of the books was a militant picture of Hitler. I tried to reason that the material probably belonged to the doctor and his family. But when I told my parents, they were seriously concerned and asked me not go there again. I argued. I wanted to be Sigrid's friend.

Eventually, we graduated. I went to the University of California, she went to Stanford University, and our paths separated. In 1938, I learned to my dismay that Sigrid had left Stanford and returned to Germany to attend a university there. This was at a time in German history when there was no longer any doubt of the virulent anti-Semitism spreading throughout the Third Reich nor any denying or excusing Hitler's fanaticism. Moreover, I couldn't understand how Sigrid could return to Germany to study at a time when intellectuals were fleeing that country. But nevertheless she went. I had never seen her again, nor had I heard about her whereabouts or welfare until the day we met at the commissary at Los Alamos.

She seemed as glad to see me as she had been back in high school days. I didn't ask her any of the questions flooding through my mind, but (as my letter shows) I did invite her to come over with her little daughter and visit me and she accepted.

I wanted to know so much. How long had she remained in Germany? What was her reaction to Nazism? What had happened to her since? How had she gotten to Los Alamos? Yes! With her history, what was Sigrid doing at Los Alamos?

We had a tense, difficult afternoon together. Sigrid was charming and friendly, but we both avoided talking about the questions that were on my mind. Her Annabel played with Bobby while we chatted mostly about our husbands and our children. I learned that Sigrid had married a man who was in the construction business. He had just arrived on the hill to work for the Zia Corporation, which had the contract for construction and maintenance at Los Alamos.

Then Sigrid left, and we didn't get together after that brief visit. I was terribly disappointed in myself that I had wasted the afternoon in idle chit-chat. I had made no attempt to learn about the years that I couldn't understand or accept. Besides, I felt that I should tell someone, somewhere, what I knew about Sigrid. Still, I hated to do it. I needn't have worried. A bored security officer, upon hearing the above story, drawled at me, "Oh, look honey, we're not fighting World War II here; we're fighting World War III." Already? World War II was barely over!

Looking Eastward

A great deal of mail had accumulated while we were at Grand Canyon. It took a while before we caught up on personal letters and correspondence concerning our anticipated move to New York. Finally, the letters and business out of the way, we poured through an accumulation of *New York Times* newspapers that had arrived during our absence. We learned that OPA (Office of Price Administration), a wartime necessity, had been terminated. The OPA had controlled prices and rationed items as necessary. Now, suddenly, there were no controls on prices even though supplies were still very limited. As a consequence, prices were rising abruptly. And I wrote:

We're so darned depressed over the end of OPA. New
York prices are up 22 percent, which will bring Lee's salary
way down relatively. And we think we can barely manage
as it is. Now Hershey, head of the I-wish-it-were-defunct
selective service, has us concerned again. The military draft
goes madly on. The draft age limit has been extended up to
twenty-nine, and Lee is twenty-eight. I still think his draft
board would move heaven and earth to get him in the
Army. They almost succeeded three times! There are *no*
occupational deferments any more. It's just ridiculous.
Isn't the war over? I have visions of spending our last
penny to get us to New York and then finding out that
Lee must become Private Fisher—and *then* what? The
world seems to be going to pot at quite a rate. If you hear
of something compact and inexpensive in a medium-sized
uninhabited planet, let us know. Enough of my crabbing.

Enough indeed! I tried to put my complaints aside, for
there were many good times ahead before we left Los Alamos.
A welcome summer stretched before us. There would be more
time to explore, time to plan our move to New York, and
time to say good-bye to our friends and to the mountains and
desert we had grown to love.

There was time, also, to seek out a writer of children's
books, whose stories I had adored as a child. He had written
wonderful tales about wild animals, about nature, about the
philosophy of the red man. I was delighted to learn through a
friend of mine that this writer, now quite old, lived near
Santa Fe. It took some sleuthing but we found him! And I
shared my pleasure in meeting my childhood idol, as I wrote:

Today's adventure was really a thrill! Ernest Thompson
Seton, my childhood hero, lives between Santa Fe and
Lamy. The place is actually called Seton Village. Well, we
located the tiny settlement and met the old guy himself. He
is a mere lad of eighty-six, tall, erect, white-haired, and he

has no wrinkles. He is very agile and completely charming. I've adored him since I was a child; nothing's changed. He spent most of the afternoon with us and was completely delightful. We got him started recounting adventures and then could hardly stop him. Then he and I had a wonderful time singing Indian songs that we both knew. We got along wonderfully. He had just written a new book, the story of his life, and he autographed one for us. Before we left, we had the dubious distinction of having Mrs. Seton, no youngster either, back her car into ours and dent our fender!

Saying good-bye to our many friends involved party after party. One of the festivities involved Leon's associates at work, as I wrote:

Lee's division had a picnic Saturday in Frijoles Canyon. I guess scientists can plan in a way that singers cannot because this time everything worked out beautifully. They even rounded up horses for us all to ride. Lee and I rode up some easy trails. Lee held Bobby in front of him on his saddle. Later in the afternoon our fun was spoiled when Marian Lebourveau, John's wife, fell from a horse down a canyon wall and broke her neck. At first, they feared she'd be paralyzed, but she is all right. She is pretty uncomfortable and all bound up, and will be for over a month. But she is really so lucky. And maybe we are too. Lee and I realized, afterwards, that we were two dummys to take Bobby along on a horse, as we are pretty inexperienced riders. One look at Marian, immobilized in the hospital, taught us not to take such chances with Bobby again.

Summer brought long hot days and a welcome surge of hopefulness at Los Alamos. The feared May-Johnson bill did not become law. This was a pleasant surprise for us on the hill. We had felt disappointed that Oppenheimer had not cooperated with Willie Higginbotham in protesting the bill. On the contrary, Oppenheimer, with other luminaries such as Robert Millikan and over two hundred professionals of Cal Tech, Mount Wilson Observatory, the University of California at Los Angeles and the prestigious Huntington Library, had signed a lengthy statement in support of the bill. This bill, if passed, would have continued to keep all the work at Los Alamos and the related projects shrouded in secrecy and under military control. It seemed to me that this law could have been an ominous forerunner of peacetime censorship.

There had been few among the older scientists who had been willing to donate time to give the alternative McMahon bill impetus. Clearly, the older men would not be leaders. They had labored too many years as detached scientists and learned their lesson of detachment too well. In fact, I. I. Rabi, Nobel Laureate and senior consultant to the Los Alamos Laboratories, commented thusly on the lack of political activity at this time, "They [the young physicists] didn't need us."

The McMahon bill passed the Senate on June 1, 1946. It was amended and weakened in the House of Representatives and finally signed by President Truman on August 1, 1946. The labs were to be transferred to civilian control and they have remained under civilian control ever since.

One battle had been won, but the concerns of the younger scientists were many. Impatient members of the Federation of Atomic Scientists were considering legitimate, legal methods of destroying stockpiles of fissionable material and of stopping bomb production. An official American plan was developed to internationalize the atomic bomb. This plan was brought to the United Nations by Bernard Baruch, a senior political figure of high reputation. In June of 1946, close to the time that the McMahon bill passed the Senate, Baruch presented the American plan to the United Nations Atomic Energy Commission.

Looking Westward

While the UN was arguing the merits of the plan, American scientists were heading again to the Pacific, this time to Bikini Atoll. Here a huge fleet of seventy obsolete ships had been anchored and here, under the aegis of the United States Navy, an atomic bomb was dropped over the fleet, and a second bomb was detonated under water. Regardless of its possible scientific merit, this undertaking was a miracle of bad timing and bad publicity if our government sincerely hoped for internationalization of the bomb.

In retrospect, it is clear that there had not been adequate preparation for protecting humans. Unfortunately, as a result of military censorship, the damage was reported as lighter than expected. This report was later corrected and upgraded, but too late to affect the initial public reaction to the news.

Actually, the preliminary news from Bikini dulled the public's reaction as it learned that two bombs had been detonated over and under the fleet. The first one (number four in atom-bomb history) was air-dropped on July 1, 1946. The second Bikini bomb was exploded ninety feet under water. The bombs, it seemed to the public, were not so bad after all. They had caused no tidal wave and had been less destructive than initially anticipated in regard to the number of ships destroyed. As a matter of fact, the underwater bomb had caused a hollow-cored column of water over 2,000 feet in diameter to shoot a mile up into the air and to fall back in a storm of steam, waves, debris, and radioactivity. Bikini was uninhabitable for years. A huge radioactive danger permeated the Pacific area. This was not generally known at the time.

Pravda, however, reported shattered faith in our intentions after learning of the Bikini tests. The Baruch plan was vetoed by the Soviet Union. Perhaps it might have been vetoed anyhow. On June 19, Andrei Gromyko, Soviet Ambassador to the United Nations, presented an alternative Russian plan for atomic bomb control that involved a mutual agreement not to use the weapon. This plan was considered unworkable and did not pass in the United Nations. (Unknown to the United States, the Russians were already at work producing their own atomic bomb. Our atomic bomb monopoly would expire much sooner than we had expected.) The brief, vain hope that the evil bomb, spawned by war, could serve peace and internationalism had died a speedy death. I felt too discouraged to write much about it in my letters, except for the following brief note.

The Bikini scientists are back—some only temporarily. It is most interesting to talk to them and very, very discouraging to learn that so much is censored, so much that people ought to know! Maybe the next "shot" will scare people into having some sense. On the other hand, maybe the whole thing is just beyond human imagination.

The horrendous experiment at Bikini was almost as upsetting to me as the slides of Hiroshima and Nagasaki had been. I felt convinced that war was no longer a rational means of settling anything. Might never did make right but, in the distant past, we could rationalize our victories—if we won. Our cause was "just" and "God was on our side." Anyway, only the combatants got hurt or killed. The red jackets lined up against the blues. Noncombatants could watch safely from a nearby farmhouse window, viewing the war practically as one might witness a spectator sport. The winner gained the land or the castle, or put his men in charge of the peasants, and life went on pretty much as before.

But World War I dragged on for four miserable years and serious doubts were raised all over the world as to the sense of the slaughter. At its conclusion, most Americans believed that the allies had fought and won the "war to end wars." The peace pact was our evidence and the League of Nations our insurance.

The enthusiasm for world cooperation did not last. The United States, experiencing a wave of isolationism once again, did not join the League of Nations. That organization gradually weakened and died. Too soon, the world was again engulfed in war. World War II shattered any illusions we might have retained of war being confined to military maneuvers. Population centers became targets, starting with the deliberate bombing of London, progressing to the saturation bombing of cities like Dresden and Tokyo, and culminating in the horror of Hiroshima and Nagasaki.

Living Americans have not experienced war on their own soil. The slaughter happened "over there." *Their* towns were destroyed, *their* lands ravaged. At the most, we put up with petty inconveniences and shortages. Our boys returned, some as they had left, others physically and emotionally injured, and still others in neat pine coffins. It was heartbreaking for families and friends, but aren't all injuries and deaths?

Lady of Hiroshima, I am sure you agree with me that Hiroshima and Nagasaki offer a grim warning to the world that warfare can no longer accomplish military objectives without side effects that destroy its original purpose. These were the thoughts that were in my mind in the summer of 1946, as we completed our plans to move to a city that I felt would surely become a prime target in any future world war.

Farewell, Los Alamos

As we prepared to move from Los Alamos, we learned that the project had come up with a basic plan of financial compensation for moving expenses. Moving allowances were offered in an attempt to be as fair to the residents as possible. The compensation plan was based upon the assumption that most of the residents would return to the general area from which they had come. That probably was true in most cases.

Los Alamos, it turned out, would pay moving expenses prorated for the same distance a family had traveled at the time they initially came to the project.

It certainly was a most logical system, but we were in trouble as a result. We had come to Los Alamos from Albuquerque, only about 85 miles away. We were moving to New York City, which is over 2,000 miles distance from the project. Therefore, we understood that the project would pay only a fraction of our moving expenses. The only sensible solution was for us to sell our furniture and take as little with us as possible. So, during our last month on the hill, we jettisoned, gave away, or sold as much of our worldly goods as we felt we could part with. Our accumulation of possessions gradually dwindled.

As our furniture was sold to newcomers on the hill, we relied temporarily on GI (government issue) furniture. I watched our old washing machine being hauled off and remembered a weeping Apolonia. Our desk was removed next. There I had spent so many evenings typing while Leon attended meetings or worked until late hours. Bobby's bed, our mattress, and springs were distributed next. Soon we were left with boxes, barrels, and cartons. The scene was reminiscent of our first weeks on the hill.

Once again, my old typewriter sat precariously on top of a barrel, my old typewriter on which I had told the story of my triumphs, challenges, and despair over these last two years. That old machine had recorded my bouts with regulations and restrictions, my delight in Bobby, my hopes and fears through my pregnancy, my difficulty understanding my husband's tensions, my mixed feelings of joy and alarm as the dreadful war ended and the peace seemed so very fragile, and my growing depression as I began to recognize that the seeds of World War III were already being sown.

One day, in the midst of our dismantling, along came a truck and crew. Two cheerful workmen waded through our

boxes and cartons and installed a telephone in our house—
just as we were almost ready to leave! And I wrote:

Great news! We now have a telephone! Our number is
503J1 and you can call us any time! It was installed yesterday. Lee can call me (and he did already!) and I can call
him. Rhuby Jean got a phone, too, and we had fun chatting
on the phone. This afternoon our toilet went out of order.
All I had to do was telephone the plumber. Life is so much
simpler now that we are ready to leave.

At this late date Los Alamos had given us, via the telephone, another connection to the outside world. At the same
time, our fading Shangri-La presented us with a reminder of
one thing we were leaving, one we definitely would not miss.
As I wrote:

The weather has turned hot. A brief but heavy rainstorm
early this afternoon hadn't cooled the air, so we put Bobby
in a minimum of clothing and let him go barefoot and
splash through the puddles. He loved it. But, you guessed
it, he fell into the mud and was such a slimy, slippery mess
from head to toe that we didn't know what to do with him.
First, I scraped him with a knife. Then, as the sun came
out, Lois came to the rescue with an iron tub. Bobby had a
public outdoor cleanup while surrounded by a respectably-
sized audience of all ages. This was followed by a real
bath in our kitchen sink and soon he was back to Bobby-
color again. I set him to work crayoning while I started
typing.

We left Los Alamos around the first of September of 1946.
The move took careful planning. Like most metropolitan
areas at that time, New York City and the surrounding
suburbs were experiencing serious housing shortages. Leon

would drive our car east and find temporary housing for us. I arranged to take Bobby and Larry to visit their grandparents in California and wait there until Leon could find a place for us to live. As soon as he was successful, our boys and I would fly east and join him.

We thought we had our departure well planned, but we hadn't counted on one last surprise from the Army. The airplane we were to board was scheduled to leave Albuquerque at 7:00 A.M. In order to reach the airport with a modicum of safety we felt we should leave Los Alamos no later than 3:00 A.M. Any civilian family leaving Los Alamos permanently was offered transportation by military car to the nearest airport or railroad station. We gratefully accepted that offer. Arrangements were made for a big Army car to be at our disposal at that early morning hour to drive us to the airport.

We were up and ready at the agreed hour, but no Army car arrived. We waited peering out into the black night for a sign of the car. We listened in the silent desert night for the sound of a car motor. Finally at 3:30 Leon called the military motor pool and learned that they had mistakenly scheduled us for 3:00 P.M. the following afternoon. We were told there was no way that a driver and car could come and get us in the middle of the night.

The gas tank in our car was only half full of gasoline. Would it get us to Albuquerque? There would be no gas stations open along the way. We didn't feel we had any choice but to take a chance that we could make it, taking a little comfort from the realization that the trip by car would be down hill most of the way.

Quickly we loaded our baggage and our two sleepy children into the car and drove off. We passed the darkened McKee houses and had no trouble passing through the inner gate. After being stopped briefly at the outer gate we headed down the curving mountain road that led off the mesa to the slumbering desert below. Then, on two retreaded tires and two that were threadbare, we coasted as much as we could down through the piñon hills to Albuquerque. We arrived at the airport at quarter to seven, tumbled out of the car and ran inside the terminal only to learn that the airplane had been delayed in Denver. It hadn't even arrived at the airport. It would be at least two hours late.

We had lived on our enchanting and terrifying mesa for almost two years. But so much had happened in that brief time that it seemed we had lived on our hill for ages and ages. We both realized that we were leaving Los Alamos as very different people from the two young innocents that had arrived at the wrong office, and moved into the wrong house, in October of 1944. We couldn't imagine that we would ever again feel as lighthearted as we had in those days long ago. As we left, we took with us the memories of bracing mountain air, fantastic landscapes, and wonderful friendships. Shangri-La was no more. We couldn't forget the experiences of laughter and solemnity, of thrills and aggravations, of hope and despair. I wonder how many left, as we did, permanently sobered by the specter of the mushroom-shaped cloud.

12. *Hiroshima—1979*

LADY OF HIROSHIMA, I have recounted for you my
experiences at Los Alamos. Do you understand now
why I wanted to tell you that I, too, was a survivor, a
survivor from the time in the past when we both had the
illusion of eventual peace and safety and the right to dream
of a future for our children and for all children?

Since the bombing of Hiroshima and Nagasaki, the world
has had forty holocaust-free years. I wonder how those
years have been for you. Can you ever remove the scenes of
horror from your mind's eye? You came to the Cenotaph
alone. Are you truly alone? Do you have children who survived the bombing of Hiroshima, and do they comfort you?
Have you been able to live with some feeling of contentment
during these years?

In the years that followed Hiroshima and Nagasaki, my
husband and I tried to live as though there is a future. We
have succeeded pretty well, and our lives have been full and
rich. We have raised four wonderful children. Our children
all are married, and we now have five delightful grandchildren. We both have had satisfying careers, Leon as a
physicist and I as a clinical social worker. Since 1961, we
have lived in California in a big, comfortable home about
forty minutes south of San Francisco.

In 1979, Leon was appointed a senior scientist in the Office
of Naval Research at the American Embassy in Tokyo. We
both felt it would be an interesting professional experience for
Leon, as well as a wonderful opportunity for both of us to
spend an extended time in Japan. Leon left his position as
dean of science at California State University at Hayward. I

left Children's Health Council in Palo Alto where I worked
as a senior clinical social worker. Together we traveled to
Japan. We left behind our children and grandchildren and also
my eighty-seven-year-old mother. We were thrilled at the
prospect of becoming acquainted with the Far East. Ahead of
us stretched adventure!

Although we came originally for just one year, that commitment was extended to three years. We continued to feel
privileged to have that opportunity. While in Japan, I worked
part-time as a counselor at the International School of the
Sacred Heart in Tokyo. I also worked part-time as a psychotherapist with the Tokyo Community Counseling Service.
Leon's work entailed travel to many parts of Japan as well
as to many countries in the Pacific area and beyond. I went
along as often as possible. We traveled all over the beautiful
islands of Japan and also visited many other Asian countries.
We also traveled extensively in Australia, New Zealand and
India. This was a rich and rewarding growth experience for
both of us. As I traveled throughout Japan and observed,
listened and learned, I came to love your country and to make
friends with many of its fascinating citizens.

Unfinished Business

Still, I had a sense, a nagging sense, of unfinished business.
Another woman, my American mother, had a lot to do with
my inability to shake that feeling. You see, she had saved
my letters, over one hundred of them, written from Los
Alamos so long ago. Time and time again, she had urged
that I prepare them for publication. But I was too busy with
family and career. I was not willing to give the time or to
undertake the concentration on the past that I felt would be
necessary to do justice to those letters. More importantly,
I didn't want to dwell on my feelings during those upsetting
days.

It was fairly early in our stay in Japan that one of Leon's assignments led him to Hiroshima, and I accompanied him on that trip. In late November of 1979, Leon and I journeyed by boat from Matsuyama, a peaceful, beautiful, three-hour voyage on the Inland Sea. Debarking at the port of Hiroshima, we made our way to our hotel located very near the Peace Park. Leon was met there by Professor Narumi, who promptly whisked him off to the physics department of Hiroshima University. I was free to visit as I pleased.

I went immediately to the Peace Park to see the burial place of the countless victims of the atomic bomb, to view the monuments to their memory and to peace, and to visit the Peace Memorial Museum dedicated to preserving the story of Hiroshima, the city vaporized by a bomb developed at Los Alamos.

I walked through the park before entering the museum. First I stopped at the Cenotaph, the arch over the stone chest that contains the "book of the past." This book identifies all known victims of the bomb. On the chest is inscribed, "Let all the souls here rest in peace, for we shall not repeat the evil." The Cenotaph is simple in design and graceful. In front were banks of flowers, some fresh, some wilted.

It was here that I observed you, the tiny, frail woman who, unaware, had moved me so. Your presence, the grim box before you and the oddly shaped Cenotaph arching over it, all seemed to conspire to start me reliving experiences long forgotten. I have told you already that I wanted to reach out to you and comfort you. You know now that also I wanted to comfort myself. As you turned and left, our eyes met for a brief second. How could you know what I was thinking? How could I tell you that I am sorry that we both live in such an insane world that could let a thing like this happen?

Woman of Hiroshima, if we could have spoken, you might have wanted to ask me a question similar to the one I had wanted to ask Sigrid. With my background and with my history, what was I doing in Hiroshima? Had I come out of

curiosity? Had I come to gloat? Had I come to defend?
I don't think you would have expected me to tell you truth-
fully that I had come to mourn. Would it have been hard for
you to understand why I wanted to tell you my story?

I left you and walked on to a mound where countless
atomic bomb victims are buried. This mass grave, simple in
design, is surrounded by a low fence. Here, again, I found
flowers and also fruit and drink for the spirits of the deceased.
Near me, a group of uniformed students stared at the mound
in silence.

The children's peace monument is called "The Statue of
the Atomic Bomb Children." At the top of its graceful, three-
way arch stands the slim figure of a young girl holding aloft
a large golden crane. This memorial honors the memory of
a young schoolgirl who had survived the atomic bomb in
Hiroshima. Suddenly, in 1955, she experienced symptoms
of radiation sickness. Fearing that she was dying, she vowed
to make one thousand paper cranes, which she hoped would
save her life. She completed her task yet death overcame her.
The monument was the result of a nationwide children's effort
to establish a memorial in her memory. It also serves to
express the children's hope that they might grow up and live
in a peaceful world, free from the threat of nuclear annihilation. Boys and girls from all over Japan visit this memorial and bring strings of colored paper cranes, brightly
symbolizing their wishes. A group of teenage boys were
there when I visited, tying up their strings of paper cranes.

I walked on deep in thought. I gazed a long time at a
statue of a teacher holding a small dying pupil in her arms,
and stood a while before another statue of a mother crouching
over her child. I found a lovely poem by Sankichi Toge. It is
inscribed on a simple monument, which was also festooned
with paper cranes. The translation reads:

Give back my father, give back my mother;
Give grandpa back, grandma back;

Give me my sons and daughters back.
Give me back myself.
Give back the human race.
As long as this life lasts, this life,
Give back peace
That will never end.

I walked over to the stark remains of a domed building,
the former Hiroshima Prefecture Industrial Promotion Hall,
which stands alone, mute and cadaverous, near the hypocenter
of the blast, a skeletal testimony of the disaster and a witness
to the calamity that befell Hiroshima. The shadow of its stairway, now a twisted mass of metal, was photographed on its
wall by the searing heat of the bomb.

I retraced my steps. The skies had cleared. My heart
lightened momentarily as I heard a group of children singing
together while they walked back towards the museum. In a
flash, my mind went back to Los Alamos and the derisive
song of the workers at the end of the war, the song which
boasted that "We'll tell Johnny we won the war." What had
we won? A balance of terror!

Once I stepped inside the Peace Memorial Museum, there
was no escape from the impact of the scenes around me.
A huge diorama depicted Hiroshima just after the atomic
bomb had obliterated the city. A ball representing the bomb
was poised menacingly above the pulverized, miniature houses
and streets. Huge panels around the diorama depicted ago-
nized people, their clothing aflame, running through the
smoke and devastation. Here I found a picture of a child
covered with burns, screaming for her mother who lies dead
in front of her. A shadow on a concrete stairway marked
where a person had been sitting seconds before being vaporized by the bomb. Another photo showed a woman, her face
streaked with tears, hunting hopelessly through the rubble.
For what? For whom?

As I walked from one scene to another, I wondered if we

are capable of learning a lesson from this terrible event. I know other cities in Europe and Japan were flattened by saturation bombing, but this was *one* bomb! I scanned the many sheets containing statistics of the catastrophe. One sheet dated August 6, 1946, listed the immediate human damage caused by the detonation. The figures coldly recorded 118,661 dead, 30,524 severely wounded, 48,606 lightly wounded, and 3,677 missing. In that town of about 400,000, only 118,613 were not wounded! It has been estimated that eventually over 200,000 were casualties of the bomb. All of this from one bomb!

So many thoughts vied for primacy in my head. Today, I realized, America's nuclear arsenal is huge. Our bombs are many times larger than the one that destroyed Hiroshima. Can Russia out-bomb us? Does it matter? We can wipe out civilization and so can they. What if heads of states were required to visit Hiroshima before taking office? What if the paralyzed United Nations would move its headquarters to Hiroshima? Would its representatives read the message of this suffering town? Would they recognize that the scars of Hiroshima are still unhealed? Would they weigh seriously the information that the Atomic Bomb Hospital continues to admit new patients and that the last victim of this ultimate expression of man's inhumanity to man is *still* to die?

These thoughts filled my mind when I accompanied Leon to the Peace Park the following morning. We retraced the route I had taken. He too felt sobered by the message of Hiroshima. Together we mounted a platform and pushed a heavy, suspended beam of wood against a huge bell. Its peal expressed our hope that this calamity will not happen again, anywhere.

But, what will prevent it happening again? We couldn't pretend that life could go on as usual. It won't. It can't. What can two people do, we questioned as we boarded the Shinkansen (superexpress train) to return to Tokyo? Join

peace marches? Support peace movements? Write? Write
what?

I was so busy, I rationalized. Busy doing what? Busy
having a wonderful time, busy holding two jobs, busy loving
everything about Japan and her charming, intelligent people.
Busy trying not to think about nuclear war. Busy forgetting
my typically World War II concept of the "fanatical Japs."
Recalling the pictures of the devastation of Hiroshima, it was
hard to remember the justifications I had tried to accept in
order to feel less guilty about our country having dropped
those horrible bombs over such a heavily populated target.
Those military and political explanations hadn't worked for
me in 1945, and they weren't helping me in 1979 as the train
sped us from Hiroshima.

The Letters

On our return to Tokyo from Hiroshima, I found a package
awaiting me, from my mother. It contained copies of all the
letters I had written to her from Los Alamos. There was also
a note from Mother containing an appeal to give her more
complete information than my letters contained. She explained
that she felt discouraged because I had not wanted to prepare
the letters for publication. She offered to do it with me or,
alternately, to try to edit them herself.

I started to read them. It was ironic reading my letters of
long ago and, in particular, reading them right after that
unforgettable experience in Hiroshima. It was not only
strange to read them, but it was difficult and painful. I wanted
to forget the Los Alamos years, which I remembered as both
thrilling and horrifying. I knew that I hadn't handled the
isolation satisfactorally up on the mesa, which I had tried to
call Shangri-La. Nor had I handled the tensions well when
I realized that my Shangri-La was no mystical escape from

the outside world. Instead, I had learned that the production
on our hill had left its indelible mark on a stunned civilization,
placing all the newly aware humanity on a new plane of
power and terror. As I read on, I saw how clearly my writing
showed the depression I struggled with during those turbulent Los Alamos days.

I wasn't eager to share my inability to handle the tensions of the Los Alamos years and the anxieties of the years
that followed. An honest appraisal of my life during those
turbulent war years would not result in my being portrayed
as any sort of heroine. Quite the contrary, I realized that if
I wrote of my impressions and reactions to Los Alamos, of
necessity I would be describing myself as a coward.

I had tried and tried to forget Los Alamos in the years that
followed, but actually I hadn't been able to forget. As a
psychotherapist I knew that it was not emotionally healthy for
me to keep Los Alamos continually alive in the back of my
consciousness and thus run the risk of having the tension and
possibly the feelings of depression affect my life. Still, I did
nothing.

While living in Japan between 1979 and 1982, I was
reexperiencing some of the isolation I had known at Los
Alamos. Here again I felt somewhat cut off from the "outside
world," due to my inability (despite language lessons) to
communicate with the Japanese. Consequently, a large part of
my life in Tokyo was circumscribed by the English-speaking
community. News from the United States seemed far away
and unreal. As I wrote to my family at home, once again
I wondered if I could convey to them the very different and
enchanting world in which I lived.

In the spring of 1980, I came home to California on a visit
from Japan. Once again, my mother urged me to go over the
letters with her. We went over many of them together.
I found myself explaining to her something of the larger
perspective I had gained with the passage of more than three
decades. Part of the tragedy, I told my mother, was that

during the war we had all been caught up in systems that had momenta of their own. The Japanese had been caught up in a powerful military dictatorship and were cast irrevocably on the road to war. Their basic sense of obedience made resistance to military control less likely. We too at Los Alamos had been caught up in a process. There was no turning back and no control of the end product of the research and development that process created. And today, the superpowers are caught up in an insane nightmarish process of building bombs in order to prevent war. Each defensive move on one side only accelerates the buildup on the other side.

Mother listened to my exposition. She suggested that I could do something about the situation. At least, she advised, I could "light one small candle for peace" by writing about my experiences at Los Alamos. Perhaps it could start some people thinking about the grim choices that face us. I listened to her but still hesitated to tackle those letters.

Back in Tokyo once again, Leon and I had many serious talks with our Japanese friends about the war years. We discussed their reactions as well as ours to the bombing of Hiroshima and Nagasaki. We told them about our experiences at Los Alamos. I shared with them some of my letters from those crucial years. We learned about the dreadful hardships of our friends and their families during the war. Several of our Japanese friends, without my asking, sent me written chronicles of their own heartbreaking experiences during those terrible years.

We faced each other across the shrinking abyss of our differing origins and lives. We agreed that war is the ultimate insanity and that the atomic bombs detonated over Hiroshima and Nagasaki represented two supremely tragic moments in the history of all humanity. Together we wondered if people everywhere could, or would, learn the lesson from Hiroshima and Nagasaki that war is no longer a viable means for settling disputes.

I listened to my friends. Encouraged by their interest, I

wrote an article about Los Alamos and Hiroshima that was
translated into Japanese and published in the Japanese
periodical *Sekai* (September 1982), and then, once again,
I put the letters aside.

In the spring of 1982, my mother came with my sister and
brother-in-law to visit us in Tokyo. We traveled together to
Kyoto, to Kurashiki, and finally to Hiroshima. There, we four
stood together before the Cenotaph. This time I felt, as I
gazed once again at the monument, that two women were
pleading with me to share my story, my mother and the
woman of Hiroshima.

On my return to Tokyo, I went over the letters once again.
As I read, so many memories came flooding back, memories
that were warm, humorous, sad, and painful. The letters
themselves seemed to record two distinctly different periods.
The first period, from the fall of 1944 to the fateful day of
August 6, 1945, recorded our turned-inward, "black-out"
years. Cut off from "normal" society during this time, we
devoted our attention to family, friends, and pet dog, and to
the endless trivia and aggravations as well as to the joys and
fears of daily life on our barren mesa above the New Mexico
desert. The period after August 6, 1945, was a time of turning outward, of reconnecting to our floundering country, to our
friends and families. The letters that followed the bombing of
Hiroshima recorded the "white-out" of the atomic bomb that
signaled the end of our isolation and the beginning of our
realization that our world would never feel safe again. We
had learned sadly that there was no going back to the idealism
of our youth. Neither was there further, temporary escape
into a cocoon like that which had initially enveloped us at
Los Alamos. It was a time of learning to live with helplessness and with anxiety while trying to raise a family in a
world that seemed destined to destroy itself. Like the struggling little band that left the fabled Shangri-La in Hilton's
story, we seemed to have suddenly aged.

I realized, as I read these letters, that I could do something concrete to overcome my own fears. At the same time I would accept some responsibility for trying to stem the drift towards a possible worldwide catastrophe. That resolve led initially to my publishing the article in *Sekai*. Following its publication, I began to organize the letters and written memories from "the hill" and to seriously undertake the task of getting my feelings and reactions on Los Alamos down on paper.

Postscript:
Los Alamos, April 1983

WHAT HAS HAPPENED TO LOS ALAMOS during the four decades that have passed? Shangri-La, which existed only in my mind, had disappeared with the end of the war. The secret home of the atomic bomb had vaporized with the dust of Hiroshima. In its place a very public community of some 6,000 lived on the mesa. Some left as soon as possible. Others lingered and waited to learn what was to happen to their erstwhile hidden community. The future of Los Alamos remained in limbo until the summer of 1946, which saw the creation of the Atomic Energy Commission and the bestowing on Los Alamos of the exalted title Los Alamos Scientific Laboratory. Los Alamos was expected to continue to design weapons and was to undertake other scientific projects as well, many that were not war-related.

Soon there were shops, stores, churches, and winding roads with sidewalks. Residents built homes in the pine forest surrounding the open mesa. A motel was built, and then another. New laboratories were scattered over several mesas and canyons. A huge bridge was constructed to span one of the steep-walled canyons. A Sears and other chain stores opened. Los Alamos began to look like a huge company town anywhere in the USA. Today, when I wander around Los Alamos, now a thriving modern community of 20,000, it is hard for me to tell which finger of land is the area we used to call "the hill."

Our oldest son Bob is a physicist at Los Alamos today. So is Minnie's older son Bill. I don't know how many children of the original residents have returned to the location of their childhood to pursue their careers. Bob, his wife, and children live in the valley below Los Alamos in a charming old house that has a long Indian and Spanish history.

The Los Alamos National Laboratory (its present title) celebrated its fortieth birthday in the spring of 1983. A two-day conference was set up to honor the occasion. Many of the original scientific and military personnel returned for the event. I decided to combine a trip to visit my son and his family with an opportunity to join in the festivities of the fortieth anniversary.

I wandered through the crowd that gathered at Fuller Lodge and quickly found familiar faces. It was wonderful to see Minnie again, now gray-haired but more beautiful than ever; and next to her, her "little Billy," who grinned down at me from his height of six-feet, three-inches. Around us was a sea of animated, elderly celebrants. We had been a young group in our twenties and thirties during the war years. Now, so quickly, we were all senior citizens! I wondered if, as we had aged, we had developed deeper insights into our various roles in creating some of the problems the world faces now. How many of us had tried to understand the momentum that drove those efforts? How many felt, as I did, that we had turned away from the social and political results of this creation and had failed to take active leadership in an effort to prevent the insane escalation of weaponry that is going on now?

I found the answer to my unasked questions the next day, in a very moving talk given by Nobel Laureate, I. I. Rabi. On the first day of the conference, Dr. Rabi, now eighty-four years old, spoke feelingly about the political apathy shown by the scientists at the end of the war. I'm sure he included himself, for I recalled that he was the man who had said, in this regard, years ago, "We weren't needed." Oh yes, they were needed, all of them!

LOS ALAMOS NATIONAL LABORATORY
40th ANNIVERSARY CONFERENCE
NEW DIRECTIONS IN PHYSICS AND CHEMISTRY
April 13–15, 1983

Wednesday, April 13

6:00–8:00 P.M.—Informal Reception at Fuller Lodge

Thursday, April 14

Main Auditorium, Administration Building

8:45 A.M.   Welcome—Donald M. Kerr, Director
Los Alamos National Laboratory
Session I—Robert Serber, Chairman

9:00 A.M.   Richard Feynman
"Tiny Computers Obeying Quantum-Mechanical Laws"

10:00 A.M.   I. I. Rabi
"How Well We Meant"

11:00–11:15 A.M.—Intermission
Session II—Donald W. Kerst, Chairman

11:15 A.M.   Owen Chamberlain
"Tuning Up the Time Projection Chamber"

12:15–1:15 P.M.—Lunch

1:15 P.M.   Felix Bloch
"Past, Present and Future of Nuclear Magnetic Resonance"

2:15–2.30 P.M.—Intermission
Session III—Edwin McMillan, Chairman

2:30 P.M.   Robert R. Wilson
"Early Los Alamos Accelerators and New Accelerators"

3:30 P.M.   Norman Ramsey
"Experiments on Time-Reversal Symmetry and Parity"

4:30 P.M.   Ernest Titterton
"Physics with Heavy Ion Accelerators"

Dr. Rabi's talk was entitled "How Well We Meant." He spoke of the World War II years as a time of greatness and folly. The greatness was manifested in our American desire to save Western civilization from being engulfed by a fanatic, barbarian culture. Science alone could save civilization. In 1943, he recalled, the allies were in terrible military shape both in the Atlantic and the Pacific.

Dr. Rabi described how Los Alamos bred a locked-up, locked-in society that seemed to turn away from happenings in the outside world and gave its full attention to the task at hand. In their free time, they enjoyed one another's company immensely. For example, the inbred group on the hill paid little attention to the liberation of Paris. Dr. Rabi recalled a parade on that day of exactly four people. He was probably right, although I don't remember any parade at all. When Germany surrendered, there was no celebration that I know of, so intent were the scientists on making preparations for "Trinity."

Dr. Rabi described his reaction to the detonation at Trinity as "visceral, it really penetrated." He was pleased for a brief moment, and then he felt covered with gooseflesh. The detonation was recognizably the "end of one world and the beginning of another." Humanity, he realized, was on a new plane of power, and the lives of the scientists—whether they wished it or not—would be changed forever. The nuclear explosion gave them a solemn responsibility that they had not expected to undertake. Feelings permeated the lab that an irreversible process had been set into motion. It was sobering to realize how vulnerable people are to what science can invent, and how helpless. The celebrations and the tensions that marked the bombing of Hiroshima highlighted this time of greatness and folly.

Folly, according to this speaker, became a thing in and of itself. We lost sight of human values. We talked as though humans were matter only.

Scientists cannot escape the responsibility bred by their

superior knowledge. Science, Dr. Rabi said, is the highest achievement of mankind. It is sinful to use it for base purposes. Now, he added, nations are lined up like prisoners of Auschwitz heading for the ovens. It is very un-American to sit around and wait for something to happen. In the past, by its example, the United States has toppled kingdoms and emperors, and asserted the greatness of the human spirit.

"We meant well [at Los Alamos during World War II]," he concluded, "but we abdicated. We cannot put the genie back into the bottle. And the power has gone out of our hands. How do we recover it?"

An overflow crowd paid rapt attention to his talk. As this very thoughtful man concluded, he was rewarded by a standing ovation. As the applause went on and on, I couldn't help but feel I hadn't been alone all those years. Many of us in that room had silently lived with feelings of guilt for responsibilities not taken, and this white-haired man had expressed those feelings for the great majority of us.

I thought of Oppie who had died many years ago. I felt that, if he had been in the audience with us, he would have felt in total agreement with the tenor of the remarks of his old friend. As I left the auditorium, I recalled my last view of Dr. Oppenheimer. I saw him last on a television program shown in 1981. It was entitled "The Day after Trinity." For that program, Oppie, grim-faced and spectral in appearance, had been interviewed shortly before his death in 1965. He was asked about the possibility of controlling atomic weapons. He answered in a rasping and tragic voice, "It's twenty years too late. It should have happened the day after Trinity." Is it really too late? Is it ever too late to try?

The solution of scientific or technical problems requires only creative intelligence and technical ingenuity, according to Victor Weisskopf, professor emeritus at the Massachusetts Institute of Technology, who was a group leader at Los Alamos from 1943 to 1946, and who was the speaker at the fortieth anniversary banquet. "The prevention of a nuclear holocaust is much harder," he said. "It requires, in addition, political and military insight, an understanding of the psychology of the adversary, and a readiness to compromise in such areas as arms control, Third World support, and common scientific projects."

On each cover of the *Bulletin of the Federation of Atomic Scientists* is the reminder "It's later than you think," and also on the cover is a clock with hands pointing perilously close to midnight. And, at Los Alamos, shortly after the war in the days when we were bitterly renaming our hill "Lost Almost," the following grim joke made the rounds:

Question: "Do you have any idea what the weapons of World War III will be like?"

Answer: "No, but I can tell you about the weapons of World War IV."

Question: "What will those weapons be?"

Answer: "Clubs!"

It is much later than we think.

Photographs provided by the courtesy of the Los Alamos
National Laboratory, Public Affairs Office, and the
Los Alamos Historical Museum are credited by
the parenthetical notation: (LANL);
(LAHM). All other photographs
are the author's own.

Main Gate. When you reached this spot, your
mountain climbing was over. You had arrived!
(LANL)

Theater II, a multi-purpose building. (LANL)

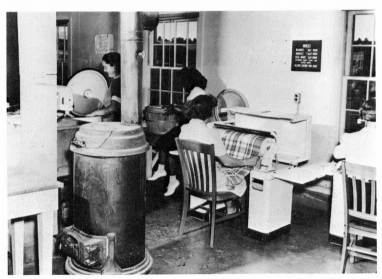

The mangle. "I tried it, and what a mess! Things looked worse than before I started." (LANL)

Mounted Police patrolled the mesa. K9 Corps dogs
patrolled the canyons below. Note evidence of the
remains of Indian cave dwellings across the
canyon. (LANL)

Bathtub row. One of the old Ranch School Houses.
(LANL)

A great military tradition blasted us out of bed at sunrise. (LANL)

The housing for construction and maintenance
workers was poorer than ours. (LANL)

A sea of mud on the Mesa. (LANL)

Mckee housing. Fences and board walks and well-built street made their appearance after we left. (LANL)

Research methods were pretty primitive. (LANL)

The entrance to the tech area. (LANL)

Inside the commissary. (LAHM)

The mess hall. (LAHM)

The Kiva (ceremonial structure) of San Ildefonso
Pueblo located near Black Mesa. (LANL)

Los Alamos Service Club for military personnel.
(LANL)

The water pipes were carefully laid above ground,
and in the winter of 1945–6 there was insufficient
snow pack to cover them. (LANL)

The water tower, our symbol of survival, was failing us. (LANL)

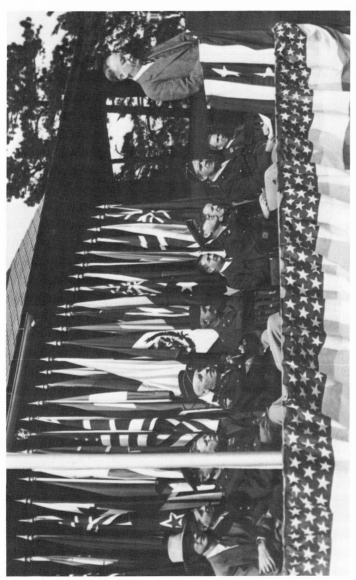

Army-Navy E Presentation. President Sproul is addressing the audience. Dr. Oppenheimer is on the far left. General Groves is behind Dr. Sproul. (LANL)

It is with appreciation and gratefulness
that I accept from you this scroll
for the Los Alamos Laboratory, and for the men and women
whose work and whose hearts have made it.
It is our hope that in years to come we may look at the scroll
and all that it signifies, with pride.

Today that pride must be tempered by a profound concern.
If atomic bombs are to be added as new weapons
to the arsenals of a warring world,
or to the arsenals of the nations preparing for war,
then the time will come when mankind will curse
the names of Los Alamos and Hiroshima.

The people of this world must unite or they will perish.
This war that has ravaged so much of the earth, has written these words.
The atomic bomb has spelled them out for all men to understand.
Other men have spoken them in other times,
and of other wars, of other weapons.
They have not prevailed.
There are some misled by a false sense of human history,
who hold that they will not prevail today.
It is not for us to believe that.
By our minds we are committed, committed to a world united,
before the common peril, in law and in humanity.

J. Robert Oppenheimer
Acceptance Speech, Army-Navy "Excellence" Award
November 16, 1945

Dr. Oppenheimer's acceptance speech, Army-Navy
E Award presentation ceremony. (*Los Alamos
Science*, Winter/Spring 1983)

The Hospital. Friends and neighbors visited through the windows. (LANL)

MPs unloading for Christmas. (LANL)

Phyllis, late December 1945.

Leon, late December 1945.

The Mesa was almost perpendicular on three sides.

Valley below the Mesa.

Black Mesa.